DZINE   *Ghost Bike* (Detail), see page 164

VELO

BICYCLE CULTURE
AND DESIGN

gestalten

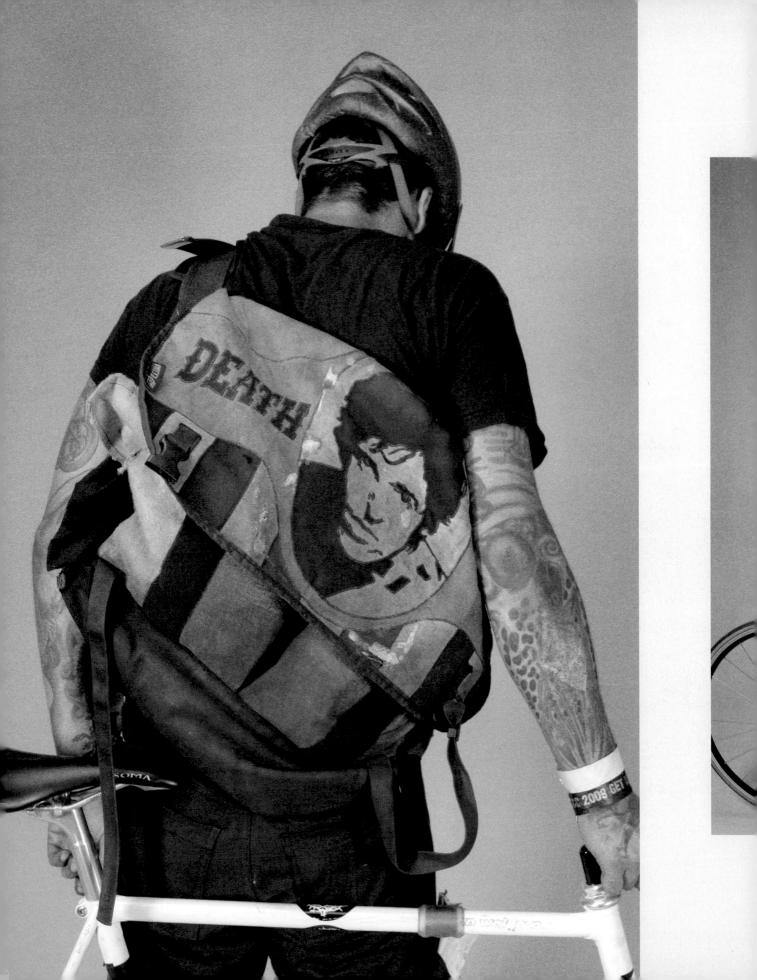

INDEPENDENT FABRICATION / NACCC / TYLER EVANS   Designer and creative director of employee-owned, Massachusetts-based Indy Fab bike manufacturer, Tyler Evans put on his photographer's hat and created portraits of cyclists at the IF checkpoint during the 2009 North American Courier Cycling Championships.

MARCO ZAMORA   Various works by Marco Zamora, 2009.

FROST PRODUKT: ALTA BIKE The Alta bike was a collaboration between industrial designers Frost Produkt, graphic design studio Bleed, and furniture designers Norway Says. Originally intended to produce a limited edition of 50 bikes, it garnered enough attention to become the first serial-production single-speed on the market. Alta is designed to be light, fast, and durable for use in the city. The brand's unique mix of creative minds also produces some unusual advertising: The latest campaign depicts ordinary people in ordinary environments with the extraordinary muscles of hardcore cyclists.

PAUL SMITH & RAPHA   In 2007 Paul Smith and
Rapha joined forces to produce an exclusive commemorative Sportwool jersey to celebrate the Grand Départ
of the Tour de France in London.

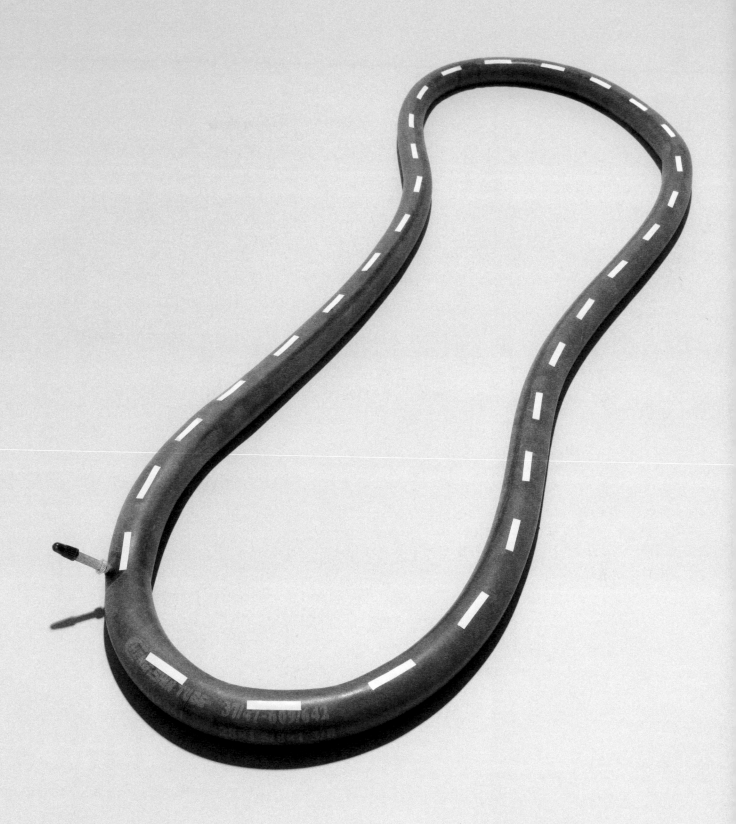

SARAH ILLENBERGER   The *Super Bicycle*
Highways illustration by Berlin-based designer Sarah
Illenberger for the *New York Times Magazine.*

PROJECT LE TOUR Texas-based Brent Humphreys'
"Le Tour" is an ongoing ambient photo study of the Tour de
France, capturing everything from the people, the performances, and the technology to the route, the subcultures,
and the passions.

ROXY ERICKSON Photographer Roxy Erickson's pictures taken during the Tweed Run event in London (2009) for Brooks Saddles.

THE TWEED RUN

BIKING MIGHT BE GOOD FOR YOUR HEALTH, BUT IT CAN DO SEVERE DAMAGE TO YOUR SENSE OF STYLE. YES, WE'RE TALKING TO ALL YOU SPANDEX-TROUSER-WEARING, UGLY-COLORED-FABRIC FANATICS OUT THERE.

Thank God for the Tweed Run, a social bike ride through the streets of London that combines a conscious appreciation of fashion with the joy of cycling. Started by freelance art director Ted Young-Ing in 2009, the Tweed Run is a fun event aimed at doing away with lycra. It has proved to be truly inspiring — some 250 people took part on its first outing and similar events now take place all over the world. Well-to-do ladies and gentlemen are pedaling through urban spaces everywhere, appropriately dressed in Harris Tweed jackets, merino wool team jerseys, silk cravats, and flat caps. Although the use of classic vintage bicycles is encouraged, all bikes are welcome. The Tweed Run also supports the Bikes4Africa charity and will soon be launching a variety of limited-edition products in collaboration with top brands — so there is clearly no stopping this wholehearted event of extraordinary class and style. Tweed the world!

ROXY ERICKSON

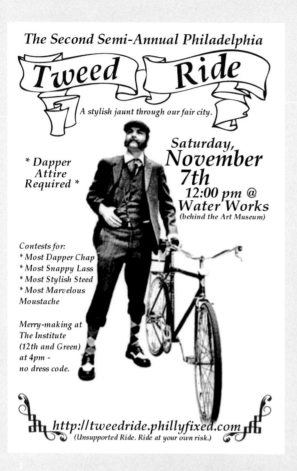

The Second Semi-Annual Philadelphia

Tweed Ride

A stylish jaunt through our fair city.

* Dapper
Attire
Required *

Saturday,
**November
7th**
12:00 pm @
Water Works
(behind the Art Museum)

Contests for:
* Most Dapper Chap
* Most Snappy Lass
* Most Stylish Steed
* Most Marvelous
Moustache

*Merry-making at
The Institute
(12th and Green)
at 4pm -
no dress code.*

http://tweedride.phillyfixed.com
(Unsupported Ride. Ride at your own risk.)

DANE COLELLA Photographer Dane Colella's portraits taken during the second semi-annual Philadelphia Tweed Ride and Flyer, a social bike ride and historic event held in Pennsylvania.

3

1

2

SIMON PEPLOW

—

Exeter illustrator Simon Peplow works for the music, editorial, publishing, educational, design, and advertising industries. He also produces exhibitions with the Outcrowd Collective, which he co-founded in 2004.

—

1, 3, 4
Exhibition piece for "Sprocket Rockets" solo show at Superb Bicycle boutique, Boston, MA.

2
Illustration for a project that involved customizing six skateboards by hand-painting them in 24 hours. They were presented to the 2012 London Olympics / Coca-Cola Activation Board.

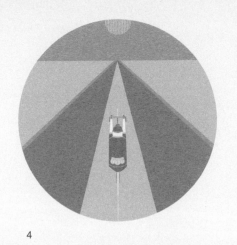

4

COPPI

5

ANQUETIL

6

MErCKX

7

PHEW

4
Limited-edition exhibition poster for the "Sprocket Rockets" solo show at Superb Bicycle boutique in Boston, MA.

5
Cycling legend — Italy's Fausto Coppi for Issue 11 of *Anorak, the Happy Mag For Kids*, published in the U.K.

6
Cycling legend — France's Jacques Anquetil for Issue 11 of *Anorak, the Happy Mag For Kids*, published in the U.K.

7
Cycling legend — Belgium's Eddy Merckx for Issue 11 of *Anorak, the Happy Mag For Kids*, published in the U.K.

8
Illustration for an article on the Braveheart Ride in Scotland by Anthony McCrossan, which featured in Issue 3 of the U.K. magazine, the *Ride Journal.*

8

opposite page
CYCLOWNS   *Cyclown Circus*, 2009, Gent, Belgium: Janski Rascal, the Cyclown Circus' drummer rides his "bass drum" bike.

1
Creating circus and music shows for kids of all ages, the Cyclown Circus travels the world with tall-bicycles, here in Jakarta, Indonesia, 2007.

2
Raffe Cataldo of the Cyclown Circus in Indonesia, 2007.

CYCLOWNS The Cyclown Circus' Anski loads up
his tall bike with busking instruments to take to town.

RANDALL STEVENS Made In Queens, 2008, New York City.

RANDALL STEVENS
WORKCYCLES /
MADE IN QUEENS
—

Randall Stevens' *Made in Queens* film documents the ambitious pedal
and decibel-pumped inventions and amped-up creativity of a group of
Trinidadian teenagers. Working late into the nights in a rented garage
on the edge of Queens, New York, they mount enormous stereo
systems and massive, blocky speakers onto ordinary BMX bikes.
Then, traveling in a pack and nearly obscured behind their moving
music boxes, they turn their neighborhood into a spontaneous — and
mobile — dance party. Stevens' film introduces us to America's first stereobike crew. They may not have produced the first Apple computer in
that garage, but the stereobike lands like a cartoon anvil on the 1970s
boombox, the handlebar-mounted radio, and the quaint neighborhood
ice cream truck.

Oaky

Mamafaka

Chubby

Gottoh

Boook

Shittak

Qatjo

Raf

33

WE ARE 2!

®©

Recoat

SPIN ON THIS

AN EXHIBITION OF ARTWORK INSPIRED BY THE BICYCLE

RECOAT GALLERY

—

An independent Glasgow gallery established by artists Amy Whiten and Alistair Wyllie in July 2007, Recoat exhibits graphic art, illustrations, photography, and street art on a monthly basis. This flyer announced the gallery's second anniversary show, "Spin on This", which focused on the theme of bikes and cycling. Artists invited to participate included Will Barras, Russell Dempster, Blackcloud, DERM, Jam Factory, Thomas Deeprose, Pone, Makinov, SYRKUS, REKOR, and design collectives WASTE and ilovedust.

SPIN ON THIS

Recoat

To celebrate Recoat gallery's 2nd birthday and 20th exhibition we asked some of our favourite artists who share our passion for cycling to produce work inspired by the bicycle

LA LABARTENDERS.CO.UK

the lansdowne bar & kitchen

www gear bikes.com

anCnoc HIGHLAND SINGLE MALT SCOTCH WHISKY

BIKE RAFFLE!

PARTY BAG FOR THE FIRST 20!

SUMS
DERM
REKOR
WASTE
SYRKUS
ILOVEDUST
BLACKCLOUD
JAM FACTORY
WILL BARRAS
THOMAS DEEPROSE
RUSSELL DEMPSTER

OPENING NIGHT:
FRIDAY 7TH AUGUST 7-10PM
THEN OPEN:
8TH AUGUST - 6TH SEPTEMBER
WEB:
WWW.RECOATDESIGN.COM
INFO@RECOATDESIGN.COM
LOCATION:
323 NORTH WOODSIDE RD
GLASGOW G20 6ND
TEL:
0141 341 00 69

JNSNP (JAO-NOO-SINGH-NAK-PAN)
The artist MAMAFAKA created this piece entitled *HEY!*

ROBB MEERTENS
—

One Halloween in London, a kid's soccer pitch became the setting for a game of polo — bike polo, that is — and graphic designer Robb Meertens recorded it on film. The biking event brought friends together in a mini tournament where competitors played in fancy dress. Prizes were awarded for the best cyclists and the most horrific costume. The group had begun playing together a few years earlier, started a league, and then hosted the European Hardcourt Bike Polo Championships in the summer of 2009. Meertens has been based in London for ten years and is an avid fixed-gear biker: "I love cycling and I also love taking photographs," he says. "I can't see a better way of traveling around the city, and when I cycle I tend to have a camera with me."

I've never felt as comfortable as I do on a bike. It just makes sense. It's simple and always there. The time spent on it is never a waste. It was only supposed to be a transportation device for me, but then I got attached. So it goes.

I saw a man who'd just been hit by a car last weekend. He was fine; could walk and nothing seemed injured. It had been just like when I'd got hit a year and a half ago: the car was turning right and didn't check his blind spot. We stopped and helped the cyclist get the car's license plate number. I was struck by just how much the driver insisted that it was the cyclist's fault and even got suspicious that the cyclist would try to take advantage and get free parts. Getting hit is scary; I was glad to be there to help.

MARISA ABAZA   Fashion Institute of Technology graduate and documentary photographer Marisa Abaza made this portrait of Amanda in Red Hook, Brooklyn for the project "New York City Cyclists". Abaza's series is distinguished from other portraiture on the subject because it includes statements, like miniature oral histories, from the New York City cyclists in the photographs.

So last week I was riding down Spring St on my way home from work. It was rush hour and I'd had a shitty day and I just wanted to cruise home at a slow pace and take it easy. So I was cruising along and some asshole sneaks up behind me in his car (or maybe I'm the asshole and just didn't realize he was there) and lays on his horn and yells out the window. So I slow to a stop and got off my bike 'cause I've had A SHITTY DAY and apparently I'm an idiot and an asshole or whatever.

FOUR dudes get out of the car And one comes at me saying he's gonna snap my neck. Alright, so I provoked them. Still...

Anyway, I got the fuck out of there and got home and drank a beer. The End.

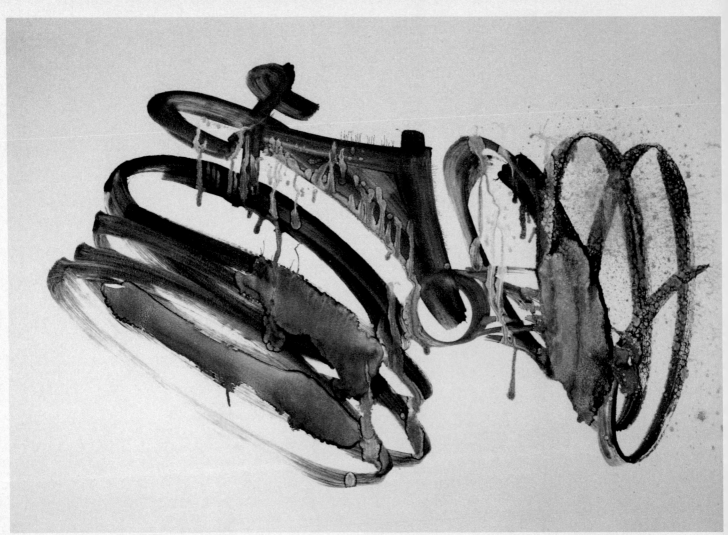

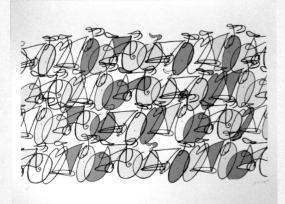

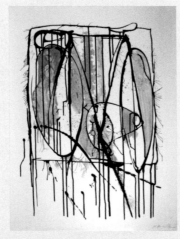

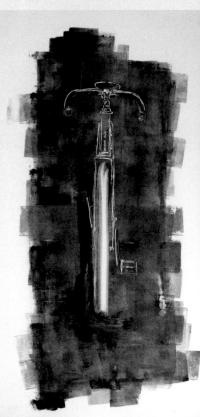

WILL MANVILLE "I ride real fast, baby, I don't ride slow," writes San Francisco-based illustrator and print-making student Will Manville. "My goal is to capture the beauty of line and pure movement, expressed through intuitive gesture." He produced this series of monotypes involving the bicycle between 2008 and 2009.

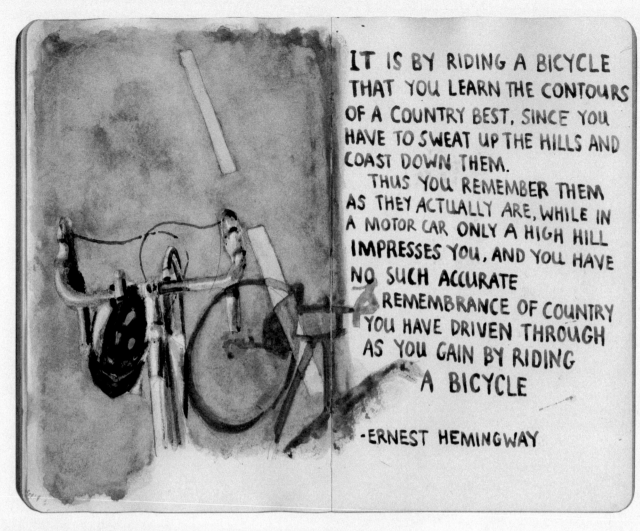

IT IS BY RIDING A BICYCLE THAT YOU LEARN THE CONTOURS OF A COUNTRY BEST, SINCE YOU HAVE TO SWEAT UP THE HILLS AND COAST DOWN THEM.

THUS YOU REMEMBER THEM AS THEY ACTUALLY ARE, WHILE IN A MOTOR CAR ONLY A HIGH HILL IMPRESSES YOU, AND YOU HAVE NO SUCH ACCURATE REMEMBRANCE OF COUNTRY YOU HAVE DRIVEN THROUGH AS YOU GAIN BY RIDING A BICYCLE

-ERNEST HEMINGWAY

WILL FREEBORN   This Scottish designer and illustrator navigates the countryside on his bicycle, taking it on the ferry to nearby islands where he draws. He produced *Where the Monkey Sleeps* (2009) at a Glasgow cafe that caters primarily to office workers and bike couriers. *Bicycles = Good* is a quotation from American author Ernest Hemingway.

MEREDITH LEWIS + ALEX NEUMAN   *Nowhere*
Soon will get you somewhere fast. NS is a bicycle tour and multimedia storytelling project that is pedaling its way from Victoria, Canada all the way to Mexico, traveling down 3,000 kilometers of North and Central American coastline. Unlike a typical bicycle tour, *Nowhere Soon* uses a portable audio recorder to document stories about local communities, networks, and people who find innovative ways "to walk the modern line between local and global." The pieces are edited on the road on a regular basis and uploaded to the website as podcasts.

KEVIN CYR *Golden light shines above* (2008), a graphite on paper drawing depicting Eddie Wang resting in the mountains.

KEVIN CYR

—

In 2008 Kevin Cyr, an artist from Williams-burg, Brooklyn whose paintings have long featured bikes and other vehicles, con-structed a cab-over camper van to attach to a three-wheeled flatbed bike. "It's probably the most fun I've ever had creating an art piece," Cyr recalls. During a previous visit to Beijing, the artist was inspired by motorized rickshaws, flatbed vans, and the *san lun che*, a three-wheeled flatbed bike. These bikes are essential for Chinese workers and used to carry anything — furniture, wood, recyclables, mounds of styrofoam, cardboard, even entire families. The Camper Bike was Cyr's way of responding to these enormous loads with an equally oversized object, and of merging something distinctly American with some-thing distinctly Chinese.

—

A 2008 photograph showing Wayne Wang riding the Camper Bike in a small village called Suojiacun on the outskirts of Beijing.

Bear your motherland in mind while casting your eyes on the world (2007), a 60 x 72 inch oil painting of the Camper Bike.

Camping far out in the wilderness forges a revolutionary heart (2007), a 12 x 12 inch oil on panel painting of the Camper Bike with rider, painted before the bike was constructed.

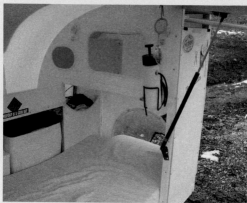

PAUL ELKINS
—

Conceptual artist Paul Elkins lives in Washington and designs and builds objects associated with minimalism and efficiency. At the annual week-long Burning Man art gathering, which takes place in the Nevadan desert and attracts over 45,000 people, only bicycles and "art vehicles" are permitted. The event's 2006 theme was "Fear of the Future," which prompted Elkins to build what he calls "a post-apocalyptic, nomadic, bicycle-towed dwelling": the Bicycle Camper. Although it may appear quaint, it was designed to withstand the harsh desert climate of the Burning Man "playa," and was equipped with almost every domestic convenience. Elkins installed a bubble skylight to let him look up at the stars in bed at night, and by day the bed folds up to serve as a comfortable chair. The entry door swings upwards to double as a sunshade and a curtain wraps around the perimeter of the doorway to give privacy when needed. In the galley kitchen, Elkins included a butane stove, food storage, a portable table that stows away when not in use, a "urinal jug," and a sink plumbed to a solar shower bag on the roof. The camper's fan, lights, and radio are powered by a 5 watt photovoltaic panel and wind turbine, which feed electricity to a 12 volt battery. The designer even constructed space for a cooler, clothes hamper and storage, and racks on which to dry food. More recently, Elkins assembled a front-wheel-drive (with freewheeling hub) tricycle, power-assisted by a 2 hp lawnmower engine. This trike now has a light roll cage covered with coroplast paneling for weather protection — and plenty of storage. You may well laugh, but it gets up to 100 mpg and putts along at 23 mph.

PEDRO REYES
—

Courtesy of Yvon Lambert Gallery, Ciclomóvil is a prototype for a human-powered passenger vehicle for Mexico City, where artist Pedro Reyes works and where there are nearly 30,000 registered bicycle taxis. Most of the vehicles on the street are self-made and have been untouched by advances in modern engineering. Reyes' concept, developed for the Museo de la Ciudad de México in 2008, has an aluminum frame, provides recumbent positions for the driver, and continues to evolve into lighter versions that include folding elements to allow drivers to squeeze into very small parking spots. The project uses Reyes' very particular notion of sculpture to explore ways of overcoming modern-day crises by increasing people's individual and collective feeling of agency.

MICHAEL UBBESEN JAKOBSEN
—

Jakobsen is a Danish industrial designer and his single-speed, coaster-brake BauBike prototype (2009) was inspired by the Bauhaus school and constructed around the geometries of the square and the equilateral triangle. The frame is pared down to clean lines and raw materials, following a set of formal rules that limit the form to straight lines in a pattern of 60 and 90 degree angles in proportions that conform to the principle of the golden section. The open-end piece above the rear wheel offers users the option to customize the function of the bike, while accessories can be placed in the tube and changed as needed.

OGYAN

—

Hiroaki "OGYAN" Okada is from Osaka and established Shukuno Rintendo, his own bike design studio which produces original bikes, in his hometown in 1994. At the same time he was also working for Kuwahara & Tsunoda, for whom he designed a jet-assisted bicycle in 1997. That same year, Okada designed a small-wheel sports bike called the Kuwahara Goblin, which earned a prize at the European Bicycle Design Contest – a first for the Japanese bicycle industry. Robin (2000) is a kit bike for children that can also be enjoyed by adults with a bit of customization. His Gaap Tour bike (2004) for Kuwahara is made for long tours, while the Gaap Wind (2003) is built for speed. From a hillside north of Osaka, Okada continues to pursue his ideal of "rin" (bike) "tendo" (heaven).

—

1
Robin, 2000.

2
Jokee, 1996.

1

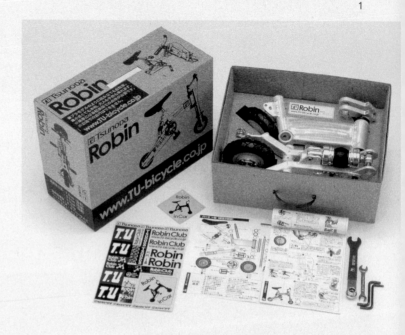

2

54

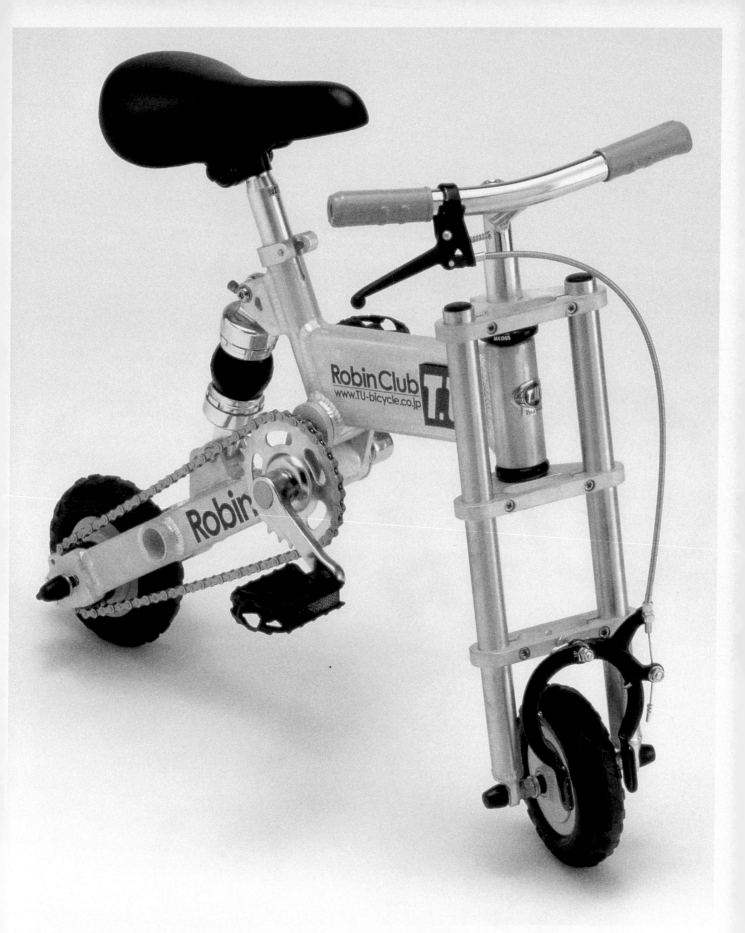

1

1
Firetrick Bob, 1997.

2
Aquatrick Bob, 1997.

3
Gaap Street, 2003.

4
Gaap Tour, 2004.

2

3

4

KOSUKE MASUDA   Cover art for Volume #5 of *COG Magazine*.

1

The *Dolder Deluxe* original model, 1977.

2

Selnau Deluxe, 2009.

3

Albisrieden Sprint, 2009.

4

Bubentraum, 2008.

5

Dolder Deluxe, 2009.

FRETSCHE
—

Zurich-based Fretsche is a high-end recycler of vintage bicycles. The company's designers generally customize bicycles whose history is already closely tied up with their owners.

WOUTER MIJLAND
—

Dutch-born Wouter Mijland works both as an artist and as a sustainable forestry specialist in Central and Western Africa, trying to deepen development cooperation between Africa and the West. Mijland's artworks are often assemblages of found objects, and his 2008 *Limousine* project — which celebrates the richness of life seen from a moving bicycle — made a stretch-limo from a bicycle, iron pipes, and paint for Generator Radsport in Leipzig. That same year, the artist made Bakfiets, a hybrid, practical creature — a satyr-like vehicle with the head of a shopping cart and the "legs" of a bicycle.

1

3

2

BIG KID BIKE
—
Metalworker and artist Greg deGouveia has built a variety of bikes and bike trailers, some to function as work horses, some for speed, and others that are conceptual in nature. As a bike advocate and bike commuter in Chico, California, deGouveia hopes to inspire others to ride more often and to try out a variety of bicycles.
—

1+2
The 2008 Kitten, photographed after its first test run, is a bike assembled from found car wheels. It weighs an incredible 93 kg and has square features, including square tubing that deGouveia used to mimic construction equipment. The Kitten also has moveable, solar-powered headlights.

3
The third prototype of deGouveia's big-wheel range, which he used to experiment with an upside-down derailleur and various steering angles.

1
Bigger Wheel 4 (2004) was his fourth big-wheel prototype.

2
deGouveia's all-terrain Jesus Lizard (2006) was built for the Arcata to Ferndale Kinetic Sculpture race. Pedaled by four people and steered by a car steering wheel at its center, it has a movable head, neck, mouth, and tail and can float with the aid of inflatable pontoons.

2

3

3
Bigger Wheel 5 (2005) was custom-built to include a seven-speed front-drive wheel.

4
The 2003 Bigger Wheel 1 was deGouveia's first proto-type of a bigger-wheeled vehicle, essentially an adult version of the beloved children's toy, the Big Wheel. DeCouveia constructed this prototype from an old bicycle frame, equipping it with both front and rear steering (although the rear steering was later disabled).

4

JRUITER + STUDIO
—

Product designer Joey Ruiter of jruiter + studio in Michigan sold his first task chair before graduating from college and now owns 25 design patents. For Ruiter, the joy of the design process "is seeing around what is expected." The pared-down beauty of his Inner City Bike, which was inspired by the hobby horse and rides like a unicycle with a front wheel attached to a bare-bones frame, reflects this fresh thinking. With shortened handlebars, a long utilitarian saddle, the ICB has been stripped of the conventional derailleur, or chain, and is powered by pedals attached directly to the hub of the rear wheel. The bike rides slowly and can be tiring over long distances: "Consider it a cafe racer with the performance of a beach cruiser," says Ruiter. But it can turn quickly and easily, features intense rear-wheel power to mount curbs and other urban obstacles, and provides great starting, stopping and sitting experiences. "What if you could find a new way to use or see things that are already familiar?" asks Ruiter, who admits he cannot wait to strip a machine down to its parts and begin again. "It creates another chapter, just when you thought you were at the end of the story."

1

REW10   REW10 Tallbike. Yokohama Special, 2009.

2
REW10 Daruma, 2009.

2

1

GOODMORNING TECHNOLOGY   Good-
morning designed the Bike Porter, a stylish take on the
traditional bike basket. The strategic design agency
discovered that, today more than ever, our choice of bike
says a lot about us: Are you a classic, a cruiser, or a fixie?
The bike market is considerably more diverse than it was
in the past, yet very few bike-parts manufacturers have
adapted to this change. They continue to develop parts
primarily for performance markets (road, track, mountain) or they make them so generic that it is impossible
for riders to express themselves. The Bike Porter, made
for people who care about style, even when carrying
groceries, is anything but neutral.

1

2

BEN WILSON   Brooks England is steeped in history, a prestigious brand founded on almost 150 years
of tradition and expertise. For Brooks, Ben designed the
Seebikesaw for (nostalgic) adults, an object that makes
strong references to the bicycle and incorporates two
Brooks products: the B33 sprung saddle and the Brooks
leather bar tape.

2

ERIC STALLER + STALLERSTUDIO
—

In 2008, Amsterdam-based, American-born artist Eric Staller of Stallerstudio introduced the Quintette, a streamlined, lightweight, more affordable version of the handcrafted, seven-person ConferenceBike (CoBi). Although all five Quintette drivers are seated in an inward-facing circle as if around a meeting table, the bike was built to handle like a sports car and features hydraulic steering and brakes, spoked wheels, and vibrant colors. Staller drew his inspiration from the sleek sports cars of the 1930s and from beach cruisers. The vehicle has been used for team-building and sports training, can climb hills, and fits on most bike paths.

Staller designed the pedal-powered CoBi (originally a seven-person vehicle) in 1991, in an effort to bring people together and to teach them to work in unison. One person steers while the other six pedal (or don't). Today, over 250 CoBis are traveling the roads of more than 16 countries. "People need this bike!" insists Staller. "People are ready to get out of their cars and off their sofas, and get a little silly! You share a moment in the outdoors, you go somewhere for an afternoon or a day, you take a picnic lunch, you move along using your own energy, renewable energy."
—

1
ConferenceBike (1994).

2
LoveBike (2008).

69

CHERYL DUNN

CHERYL DUNN IS A NEW YORK ARTIST, PHOTOGRAPHER, AND FILM-MAKER. HER WORK, AN ASSEMBLAGE OF DRAMA, IRONIC COMEDY, AND DOCUMENTARY ELEMENTS, EXAMINES NEW FORMS OF EXPRES-SION GENERATED ON THE STREET AND BY YOUNG PEOPLE, INCLUDING GRAFFITI, SKATEBOARDING, AND BIKE CULTURE.

Dunn worked for many years as a commercial photographer before moving into fine art and film, and now exhibits her work nationwide and participates in local and international film festivals. In 2002, Dunn completed a residency at the Wexner Center for the Arts and produced the documentary *Licking the Bowl* about a sculptural project using skateboarding forms created by Simparch, a Chicago-based artist collective. In 2005, she screened her film, *Bicycle Gangs of New York,* alongside an installation of portraits taken of cyclists around the city, showing members of the unicycle club and of the Puertan Rican Schwinn Club, and riders of swing bikes, delivery bikes, and cruisers. Dunn makes portraits of bikes as often as their riders: recumbent bikes, double-deckers, and frames stripped bare while locked helplessly to a parking sign. The docudrama, which later played at the Tribeca Film Festival, was accompanied by a 60-page book depicting the creativity and empowerment of the hardcore bicycle subculture of New York City, including gangs like Black Label, tall-bike riders who sport gang colors; the Landlords, who travel by track bikes with Krylon paint in their packs; the Bicycle Cherries, who wear soiled party dresses with chains; and the Denim Venom rockers. —

All images taken from *Bicycle Gangs of NY,* 2004.

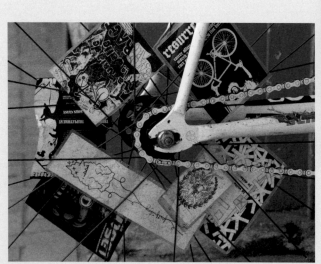

4

6

5

ROBIN LEY

1

Ley built this bike in 2009 and photographed it suspended by mono-filaments from some pipes in a parking garage to create the illusion of levitating.

2

Spoke cards on the rear wheel of a fixed-gear bicycle in the Queen Anne Light Sculpture Park, Seattle, Washington.

3

A rider prepares for the start of the Dead Baby Downhill.

4

Cyclists Chase Wreyford (left) and Ryan Wreyford (right) during the 2009 summer solstice all-night alley-cat race as they pass through the I-90 bike tunnel in Seattle, Washington.

5

Ley captures the moment before impact between two tall-bike joust-ers during the 2009 Dead Baby Downhill, a bike race and party in Seattle, Washington.

6

A tall-bike jouster prepares for combat at the Dead Baby Downhill.

RADIATOR ARTS Fantastic bicycles designed by
Radiator Arts' Adam Thompson at Skyride London 2009.

JNSNP (JAO-NOO-SINGH-NAK-PAN) *Man BMX* by BR&NDBOOK, 2009

WOON   U.S. street artist Swoon's *boy-on-a-bike* graffiti.

AEOLIAN RIDE

—

Brooklyn designer Jessica Findley founded Aeolian Ride, a gathering of 52 people who ride bicycles through cities around the world — from Santa Barbara and Bridgeport to Lisbon and Tokyo — wearing wind-inflated suits. Findley says the unusual ride was inspired by "a love for bikes, city cruising, Critical Mass, costumes, silliness, and things that inflate." Aeolian Ride is a free event that reflects Findley's dry wit and innovative energy. The suits are handmade from ripstop nylon in three styles designed to inflate at low speeds. When worn, they make the 52 riders resemble a bank of swooshing clouds descending on the city. Findley also received a grant from the Brooklyn Arts Council to create the Aeolian Ride Rainbow Edition for young cyclists that will involve more colorful costumes for kids.

AEOLIAN RIDE

MONOVELO
—

China has taken that beloved toy, the Big Wheel, and given it new meaning. As seen — glowing and rolling hypnotically — during the closing ceremony of the 2008 Beijing Olympics, the Monovelo is made up of an ABS plastic wheel, a large rubber tire over a steel frame, and, in one version, white or colored LED lights. It weighs 52 kg, measures 2 meters in diameter, is powered by a single rider (with a good sense of balance), and can reach speeds of up to 20 kmh. The Monovelo is rumored to have been inspired by the Beijing National Stadium (dubbed the "Bird's Nest"), which was designed by architects Herzog & de Meuron. Great for exercise or a short commute, it is currently being marketed as a mobile advertising platform.

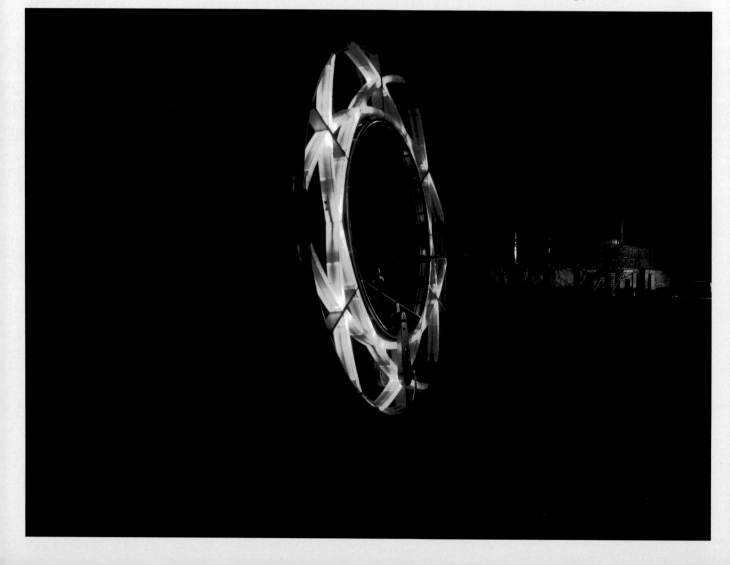

FIXIE SHIRT

—

Fixie Shirt is a small group of graphic artists in Berlin who, in collaboration with Brussels-based bike messenger service Pedal, have developed a clothing line dedicated to fixed-gear riders. Their T-shirt collection features reflective type to combine aesthetics and safety. "We want to offer handlebar freaks the opportunity to make themselves visible in aggressive urban traffic without having to look like a Christmas tree," Fixie says.

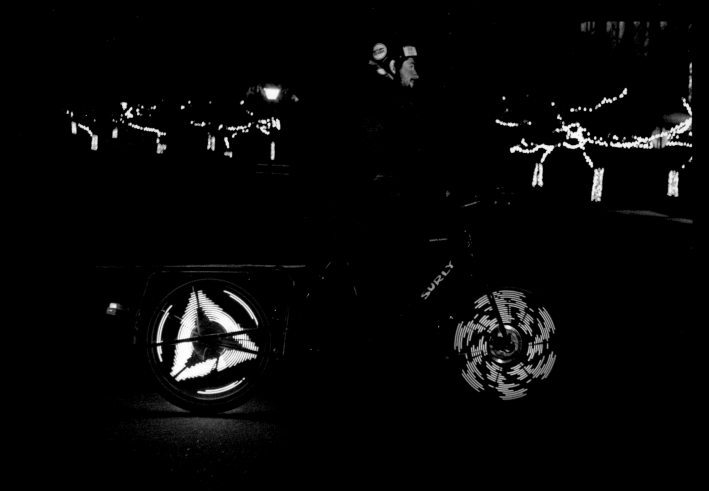

MONKEYLECTRIC   For every cyclist who feels just a little less safe on the streets after dark: The MonkeyLectric Monkey Light is a light that can be mounted to the spokes of any bike and keeps riders not just visible, but hypnotically visible. The Monkey features 32 full-color LEDs, kaleido-scopic visual effects and a tough all-weather design that will go uphill in the rain much better than you.

EMCEE C.M. MacMullan built The Moving Picture Show (2004), a tricycle outfitted for urban exploration. The Moving Picture Show module allows the rider to project 16 mm films (often Charlie Chaplin movies) on his back while riding, encouraging viewers to follow him, kind of like the Pied Piper.

BEN WILSON In 2009, Ben was one of three artists to be awarded commissioning money to create a mobile work of art which would join an existing group of vehicles for Walk The Plank's Illuminated Art Car Parades. Wilson's *ARTIKCAR* was inspired by a child's wooden toy car. The pedal-powered, illuminated vehicle is made of steel tubing and is steered by leaning.

1

1
JNSNP (JAO-NOO-SINGH-NAK-PAN)
Oaky Jew created the *Fucking Lane Of Dead* in 2009.

opposite page
The *Otaku Bike* by Rukkit Kuanhawate was commissioned by
Bangkok-based client Ride a Life.

GERHARD STOCHL   Photographer Gerhard
Stochl creates portraits of New York City cyclists in situ,
suggesting that riding a bike allows even locals to experience their territory from a completely fresh perspective.

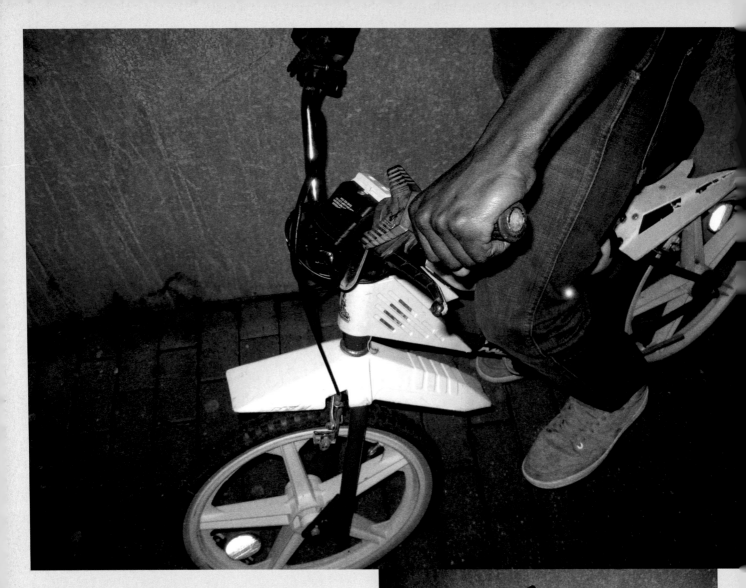

ADAM TICKLE

—

The Raleigh Vektar makes a virtue of being outdated because it so boldly records a particular moment in pop-culture history. It is as much an ode to the BMX as it is to the late 1970s and early-80s TV series, *Battlestar Galactica* (or to the speeder bikes of scout stormtroopers in the *Star Wars* movies). The BMX-like bicycle was manufactured in Nottingham, U.K. by Raleigh and featured a short wheel base and blocky, plastic-clad tubes. The plastic console on the crossbar housed an "onboard computer" that gave the rider readings of elapsed time, distance traveled, and current and maximum speed in what would become a paradigm of the old-school red LED digital display. Optional add-ons to the fabulous three-speed, battery-operated folly included a computer module accessory pack with trip meter, a speedometer, a radio accessory pack with three preset AM stations, and a synthesizer featuring eight space-age digital sounds and speakers fitted beneath the console behind the head tube. This beauty was photographed by London-based graphic designer Adam Tickle for his blog, thingsiveseen.com.

ADAM TICKLE   Shot in Redchurch Street, east London. The *Bike Lock Up* project was realized by the East London Bike Community.

KOSUKE MASUDA   Masuda exhibited his
Shimano Dura Kabuto illustration at the "Bridgestone
Cycle Art Exhibition" in Tokyo.

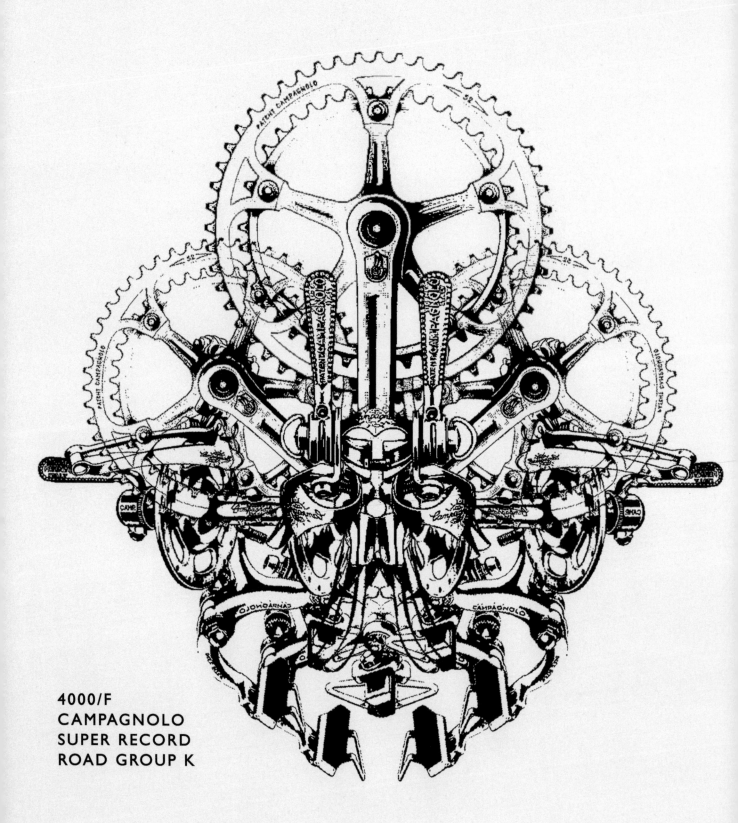

**4000/F
CAMPAGNOLO
SUPER RECORD
ROAD GROUP K**

CARRERA

MARCO

RENAULT

LAURENT

BIANCHI

BIANCHI

FELICE

KAS

FUENTE

LA VIE CLAIRE

ROULEUR

LA VIE CLAIRE

GREG

MOLTENI

MOLTENI

EDDY

RICHARD MITCHELSON   Brighton-based cyclist, illustrator, and animator Rich Mitchelson made these T-shirts for *Rouleur* magazine in 2009.

J. ADELAIDE MÉTIVIER

—

J. Adelaide Métivier's husband is very much a part of the fixed-gear bike community in Philadelphia and this tends to seep into her photography. She made this portrait of the Bearded Madman, aka Dane Colella, at the 2008 Tussle at the Trestle, an obstacle-course race held on a field under a train trestle in West Philly. Colella was tearing through the course on a "beater," an old, clunky bike. Racers had to carry their bikes over low walls, navigate a spiral and some hard turns, and try not to wipe out on the muddy patches of grass littering the improvized track.

PASCULLI Pasculli frames are named after mountain passes and villages in the Italian Apennine Mountains. The use of color is characteristic of Pasculli bikes. Clients can choose from five designs in six different colors.

PASCULLI Bicycle frames are handcrafted at the Pasculli factory in Italy. In this picture, the varnisher checks a finished frame.

FORMPASCH
—

Research has shown that — clumsy as it is — most city cyclists carry bike lights and a pump with them whereever they go. In response to this inconvenience, Freiburg-born, London-trained, Nagoya-based designer Kai Malte Röver of Formpasch created the PUYL bicycle pump and integrated light. The design won him the 2009 iF Design Award and EUROBIKE AWARD. PUYL combines the two pieces of equipment into one device and is the first permanent bicycle light that does not require a battery. Röver's idea is based on Faraday's law of induction but, in lieu of batteries, it uses electromagnetic induction. The electricity is generated by moving the compressor/magnet through two copper coils that are located around the inner compression tube, meaning that the light's battery is charged while pumping. The energy generated is stored in a rechargeable battery, or super cap, to illuminate an ultra-bright LED. The magnetic recharge method has the advantage of allowing the LED to be recharged an unlimited number of times. Another clever trick: Röver used parts designed to endure long use and abuse and reduced the mechanical components to a minimum.

RAPHA
—

Rapha was launched in 2004 with the aim of celebrating road riding and of developing the best performing and most stylish cycling clothes and accessories in the world. Since that time the brand has not only released some of the most beautiful pieces of performance clothing around, but has also become a hub in cycling culture through activities such as the quarterly magazine *Rouleur,* the Rapha Condor team it established in 2006 with London-based Condor Cycles, and the Nocturne Series that has been held every year around the historic Smithfield Market in central London since 2007.

Inspired by gentleman riders of the 1930s, this suit is the result of a 12-month collaboration between British tailor Timothy Everest and performance cyclewear label Rapha. The two joined forces to bring sartorial elegance to the urban commute. A fitting balance of ergonomics and aesthetics, the three-piece cycling suit meets the needs of the city cyclist who requires his attire to move easily from the bike to the boardroom. As well as a ready-to-wear option, bespoke suits are available to meet exacting requirements on fit and detailing.

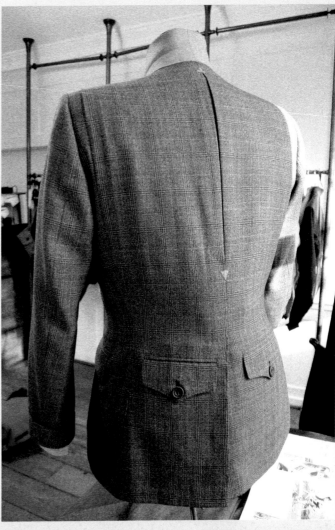

DASHING TWEEDS   Dashing Tweeds designer
Guy Hills created a women's bicycle cape from reflective
material.

MICHAEL EIDE   Danish-born Michael Eide has created a dual concept with his YAKKAY bicycle helmet: one helmet, various covers. By attaching different covers to the helmet, users can change the look and feel of the object, turning it into a cap, for example. The size of the helmet can be adjusted using adhesive foam circles, which also allow air to circulate inside the helmet and keep your head cool.

2

HOUSE INDUSTRIES
—

House Industries is a Delaware-based independent type foundry, illustration studio, and design firm that supplies unique fonts and artwork to the advertising and design industries. The company also sponsored the 2009 season of the cyclocross team of racer and renowned bike manufacturer Richard Sachs.
—

1

Kaisa and Christoffer Leka are avid bike tourers, which in itself is not remarkable, except for the fact that Kaisa is a double amputee. House Industries geared them up in wool cycling jerseys for a ride on the quiet roads near House's Delaware studio.

2

Renowned bicycle manufacturer Richard Sachs and his wife, Deb, staff the bike pit during the UCI Elite cyclocross race near Wilmington, Delaware. Sachs keeps out the chill of a late autumn rainstorm with a House Industries Merino wool zip trainer.

3

The foundry's wool cycling team kit was designed for its own cycling team, who needed a kit for both home and away races. It is a simple chain-stitched embroidered wool uniform. The Merino wool actively wicks sweat away, eliminating odors for post-race comfort and "plenty of rap with hot bicycle bunnies."

4

The operators of the Velocipede Salon (www.velocipedesalon.com), North America's most successful cycling forum, commissioned House Industries to create a new logo and identity for their growing empire. "Unfortunately," a House representative says, "the creative brief cross-pollinated with several of the multi-legged anthropods that inhabit the studio."

3

4

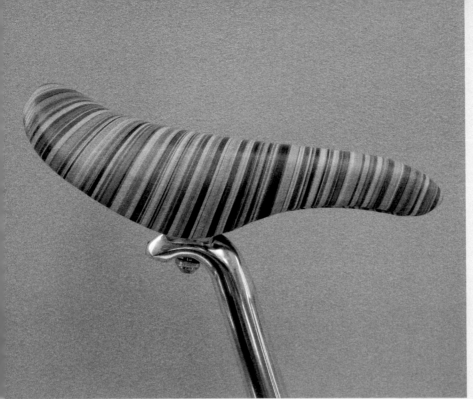

PAUL SMITH
—

Among the many things there are to know about the British fashion designer Paul Smith is that he was once a serious cyclist. Smith fell into fashion at the tender age of 17 because a bike accident put an end to his hopes of becoming a professional racer. Smith used to ride a Mercian through the Derby countryside and still owns that bicycle today. In the winter of 2006 he teamed up with the Derby-based bicycle makers and personalized two Mercian models: a track bike and a tour bike. The Paul Smith for Mercian bicycles are available in six vivid (of course) custom-made frames. In 2007, to celebrate the Grand Départ of the Tour de France in London, Smith, through Paul Smith Jeans, also teamed up with bicycle gear retailer Rapha to produce an exclusive commemorative Sportwool jersey and a range of tweed and houndstooth cycling caps.

—
1
Paul Smith Kashimax saddle.

1

DAN FUNDERBURGH
—

Dan Funderburgh, a Brooklyn wallpaper designer and artist, makes patterns, prints, and installations that shout out his passion for the decorative arts and his disdain for the popular division between art and decoration. His pieces incorporate influences ranging from 14th-century Moorish mosaics to 60s op art, and can be found in the collections of the Cooper-Hewitt Design Museum and the Miami Museum of Art.

—
2
L'Alpe d'Huez Pro Saddle (2009), a limited-edition saddle for the Brooks Team, is hand-embossed with a topographic map of the Tour de France mountain stage, l'Alpe d'Huez.

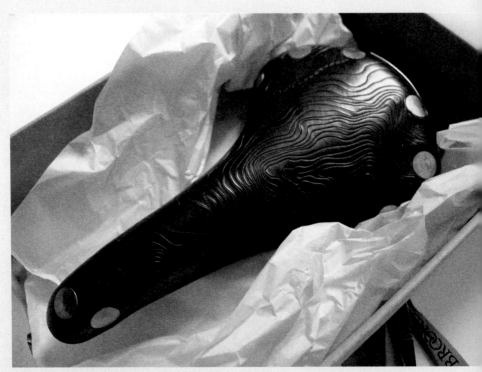

2

KOSUKE MASUDA

—

Artist Kosuke Masuda, also known as Ko, lives and works in the Shingon Esoteric Buddhist temple in Yokohama, Japan.

—

1
Engraved Sunstar hub.

2
Carved Brooks saddle.

3
Engraved bike parts.

4
Engraved aluminum bike frame.

5
LAURA CRAWFORD   Laura Crawford is a metalsmith, artist, and "bicycle traveler" from Corvallis, Oregon. She creates jewelry and bike accessories that celebrate our connection to nature. As part of the "Path Less Pedaled" project, she traveled the world by bicycle, making objects along the way. She hand-crafted the copper *Bike Moustache* (2009) in Long Beach, California as a whimsical adornment for head tubes the world over.

DAN FUNDERBURGH   The one-color
screen-printed *New Hope Assembly of God* (2008).

1

2

1

CYCLE WORKS A classic biking item, this is CWO/Beloved Cycles' version of the cycling cap.

2

MARIE-LOUISE GUSTAFSSON Marie-Louise Gustafsson is a Swedish product designer and graduate of the Royal College of Art and Konstfack. Her conceptually pragmatic designs have been shown around the world. Her "granny-chic" bike basket Carrie (2007) for Design-HouseStockholm was inspired by her grandmother's crocheted tablecloths and by working out the best way to take a coffee break out in the country. It can be used as a shopping basket, a picnic basket, or turned upside down to form a quick-fix picnic table.

3

GUU-WATANABE Frontbag Sakura.

3

GUU-WATANABE

—

Craftsman and designer Watanabe Shoichi and his assistant Tomoko started Co.Ltd guu-watanabe in the mid-80s in Tokyo, making custom-designed bags and bike bags. The quality is in the details — they polish the edges of the leather with sea cucumber and starch. Before sewing the bags together, they "draw" each line in with an iron. "We make a bag that we would want," says Watanabe.

THE K.I.D.S. AND SECRET SCHOOL
—

The bicycle seems to naturally work its way into any project focusing on art, health, or community improvement. K.I.D.S. is a group of Brooklyn-based guerilla street artists committed to approaching life with wonder, boundless energy, and excitement. K.I.D.S. organizes events and actions in public spaces around New York, including: pep rallies for commuters, a "high-five demonstration circle" and dress-up party, a gathering at which guests made PB&J sandwiches blindfolded, a text message theater, and a balloon parade.

—

1

In 2009 K.I.D.S. created a custom tarp made from discarded umbrellas to camouflage and protect the MOBILIZE tricycle, his "urban exploration machine," while parked.

2

K.I.D.S.' ongoing partnerships with Secret School have included a conversation about statelessness, the creation of a model economy based on the gold standard, a food-for-art exchange, and crafternoons. Growing a Network of Secret Gardens: the *Greenhouse-a-Go-Grow project-on-wheels* lives on the sidewalks of New York and reclaims public spaces for food production using a mobile garden. The plants in the greenhouse are tended by neighbors and friends in a growing network of urban gardeners.

2

The Portable Pantry (2007) was a module for collecting and preparing edible wild plants found on the streets of New York and for sharing them as a common resource with passers-by. The module was part of MOBILIZE, a tricycle outfitted for urban exploration.

DESIGN BY MUSIC
—

In 2009, commissioned by international design journal *Grafik*, Manchester-based design agency Music teamed up with Manchester BMX Club and British Cycling to produce limited-edition posters that were exhibited during the London Design Festival. The designs involved young riders from the local BMX club. The agency wanted each poster to be unique, so they used the imprints left by BMX tires as the basis of their design. Each poster was signed by Olympic 2010 hopeful Shanaze Reade and all profits go to the British Paralympic Fund (www.paralympics.org.uk) and the charity Right To Play.

MARK JENKINS   *Spokes,* a mixed-media sculpture
by American artist Mark Jenkins.

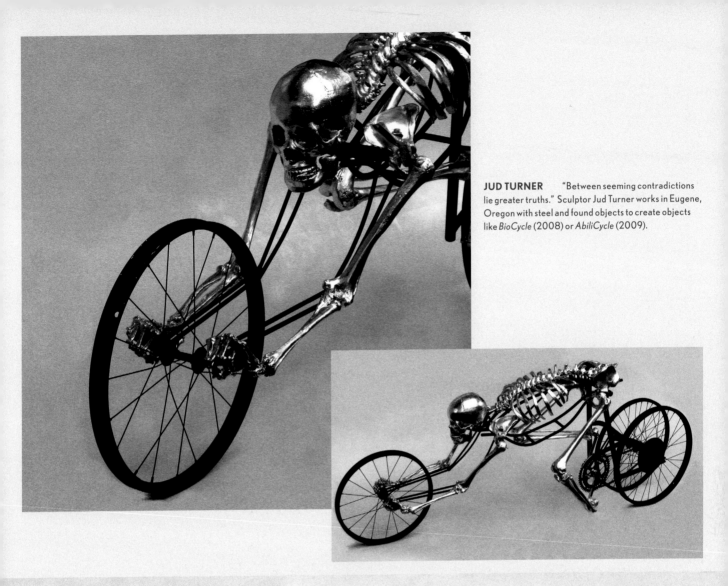

JUD TURNER "Between seeming contradictions lie greater truths." Sculptor Jud Turner works in Eugene, Oregon with steel and found objects to create objects like *BioCycle* (2008) or *AbiliCycle* (2009).

1

JONATHAN BRAND   To create his *Fallen*
(2007) sculpture, Canadian-born, Brooklyn-
based artist Jonathan Brand constructed a device
based on a drawing pantograph (entitled *Battle
Axe*) and built a wooden copy of his childhood
BMX by physically tracing the original bike, piece
by piece. A router copied the movement of his
hands, carving a scaled-down version in MDF as
he sketched the original. Fallen was cut from a
single sheet of MDF and assembled so that each
part moves freely.

2

CHRISTINA OH   "If a pencil is my favorite
thing to hold, a pair of knitting needles is a close
second," says Los Angeles illustrator Christina
Oh. "I knit for the tactile experience of giving
form to transitory thoughts that hold personal
meaning."
She hand-knitted this 5 x 7 inch bicycle using miniature double-pointed 1.0 mm knitting needles
and off-white crochet thread. She made the bike
to represent her childhood memories of cycling to
the park every day.

CHRIS GILMOUR Chris Gilmour created his life size *BIKES* in 2003, made of cardboard and glue.

MARCO FACCIOLA   16-year-old high school student Marco Facciola constructed this wooden bicycle to fulfill a class requirement. What started out of enjoying woodworking, turned out to be rather ambitions engineering project.

JNSNP
(JAO-NOO-SINGH-NAK-PAN)
—

Jao-Noo-Sing-Nak-Pan is one of the many passionate fixed-gear bike communities in the world. JNSNP is based in Langsuan, Bangkok, where members organize bike-inspired art projects, like the 70-piece "Ride a Life" exhibition. The event drew more than 500 people to the Art Gorillas Art Gallery in Siam Square, where the organization also hosted a track race and trick competition.

"Ride a Life", Thailand 2009.

JASON KINNEY Jason Kinney is an artist and photographer from Portland, Oregon. He submitted this piece for the "ARTCRANK Portland 2009" bike poster show held at the Ace Hotel.

129

50

"Fixie Death Trap"

Wasteyourself 2009
Recoat Gallery - Glasgow

**NORMAN HAYES (WASTE) WITH DANIEL LOWE
(DLOWE)** *The Fixie Death Trap* was a collaborative
project consisting of a set of two full-sized screen-printed
bike wheels mounted to the wall with a black-tape frame and
accompanied by a limited-edition silkscreen. Both were exhibited in the "Northern Exposure" exhibition at the Recoat
Gallery in Glasgow.

MARCO ZAMORA   Marco Zamora created this installation in 2009 at the FIFTY 24PDX Gallery for his *"Give & Take"* solo exhibition. This black-and-white sculpture features hints of color and is made of objects he traded with Portland residents. It formed the center-piece of the show.

MICHAEL DELUCIA *Of Primitive Means*, 2009. Bicycle, wood, plaster.

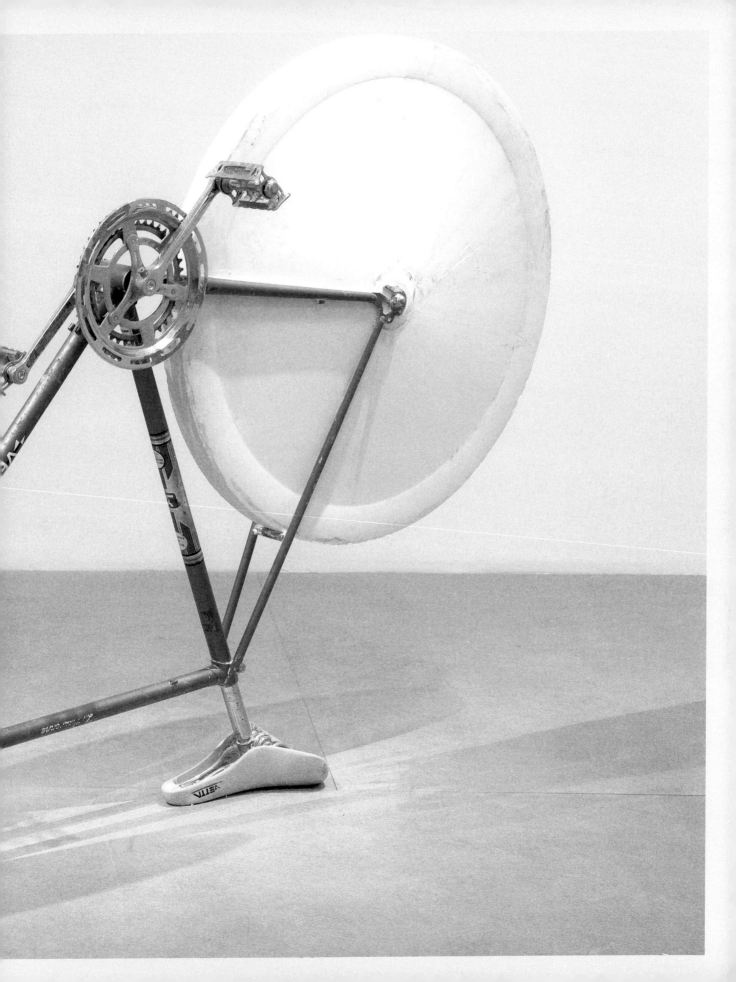

ALLAN YOUNG Allan Young, a resourceful designer based in Palmyra, Virginia, makes handsome stuff from less handsome stuff. In 2009 his reinventions included a clock made from a bicycle gear crank. Now any time is time for a ride.

134

FOLDING WHEELS

—

Folding bikes are the problem-solvers of urban transportation, making commuting, storage, and security a breeze. Despite the vast choice of folding models available today, the designs are still subject to the same constraint: wheel size. The trick is to balance portability with performance, something that the Brompton folding bike achieves very nicely. But what if you could fold your full-sized wheels up with your bike? The crossbreed wheel was designed and is under further development by London-based Duncan Fitzsimons (a member of Vitamins design col-lective) in collaboration with InnovationRCA lab at the Royal College of Art. Crossbreed wheels enable a full-sized bicycle or wheel-chair to be folded into a compact package that can be put in a bag for easy transport and storage. This means that a wheelchair with crossbreed wheels can fit into the trunk of a Smart car, a closet at home, or an overhead compartment on an airplane. Fitzsimons has developed steel and carbon-fiber concept models on which, at the flip of a lever, the rim separates into six sections and collapses into a convenient double-cylinder size.

THE WATER CYCLE /
1 PRECIPITATION > **2** RUNOFF FROM STREAMS & RIVERS > **3** STORAGE OF FRESHWATER > **4** GROUND WATER STORAGE > **5** SURFACE RUNOFF >
6 EVAPOTRANSPIRATION > **7** OCEAN STORAGE > **8** EVAPORATION > **9** STORAGE IN ATMOSPHERE > RESTART AT STEP 1

1

1
MATT COLEMAN   A graphic artist raised in the
Midwest, Matt Coleman currently lives in Pennsylvania
Dutch Country with his wife and their two bicycles.
His illustration *The Water Cycle* (2008) depicts one of
nature's most amazing processes — in the most literal
manner.

2

2
THE BUNGALOO   *Stork Legs on a Penny Farthing,*
2008.

opposite page
THE BUNGALOO   *The Last of the GhettoBlasters* is
a hand-pulled screen-print by St. Louis illustrator John
Vogl, aka The Bungaloo, for "ARTCRANK, A Poster
Party for Bike People."

COPENHAGENIZE

A DANISH CONSULTANCY BASED, YES, IN COPENHAGEN, ONE OF THE MOST AVID CYCLING CITIES IN THE WEST. COPENHAGENIZE PROMOTES CYCLING AS A POWERFUL TOOL OF URBAN PLANNING, CITY, AND HUMAN HEALTH.

Copenhagenize Consulting is based, unsurprisingly, in Copenhagen, one of the most avid cycling cities in the West. It promotes cycling as a powerful tool of urban planning and urban and human health. Copenhagenize Consulting is the result of a merger between Zakkamedia, which runs the blogs Copenhagenize.com and CopenhagenCycleChic.com, and Monoline, a communications firm specializing in urban spaces. Monoline was founded by Troels Heien, an architect, graphic designer, and photographer who studied at the Royal Danish Academy of Fine Arts. Heien runs Copenhagenize Consulting with Mikael Colville-Andersen, a documentary filmmaker, photographer, and journalist. They investigate and promote the power of the pedal, calling the bicycle "a fantastic tool for transforming cities and towns into more livable urban spaces." "My involvement in bicycle culture started by coincidence," says Mikael on how he got the bike rolling. "When you live in the world's cycling capital and ride your bike around every day with 500,000 fellow citizens, you don't notice bikes. You just use them. One day in 2006 I took a photo of an elegant Copenhagener on a bicycle in the morning light. It proved popular on Flickr and I started taking some more. That's what led me to start the now-famous Copenhagen Cycle Chic blog and then the Copenhagenize blog. It is still amazing to me to think that one photo of something as uninteresting as a Copenhagen cyclist launched a global movement and the imminent return of the bicycle as a feasible, acceptable, and respected form of transport in cities around the world. It's humbling and thrilling all at once."

The company specializes in a range of services, including marketing, branding, and campaigns; developing bicycle plans for cities and towns; designing cycling infrastructure; performing impact calculations for health and health economics; and planning bicycle parking and bike-share programs. Copenhagenizing, a term coined by Danish urban planner Jan Gehl, offers a model for cities to tackle air and noise pollution and the rising healthcare costs of lifestyle illnesses by implementing better pedestrian and bicycle facilities. "The popularity of the term Copenhagenize shows that the world needed some kind of catchphrase for where we are, and should be, heading with regards to creating livable cities, with a focus on reestablishing the bicycle in the urban landscape. Copenhagen is an inspiration on so many fronts, but the bicycle is a symbol for what is possible. Forty years ago the bicycle was fading away, but visionary political decision-making and urban planning reversed the tide of car culture. What happened in Copenhagen can happen anywhere, and if branding it as 'Copenhagenizing' helps it happen in other cities, then that's brilliant. Copenhagenizing is, however, nothing without 'cycle chic' and vice versa. It's about infrastructure, certainly, but it's also very much about marketing cycling as a normal transport option instead of an adrenaline-based sport or recreational activity."

The concept redirects urban transport to walking and pedaling rather than driving, in order to promote street life, protect the environment, and increase health and fitness among the population along with the quality of city life. "The main movement that we're seeing around the world is a return to planning our cities for the people who inhabit them as opposed to the cars they drive around in. Our urban centers were originally designed by and for pedestrians, and urban planners are now going back to our roots to explore the simple, yet powerful effects of urban mobility: planning for people with the goal of creating livable cities." This concept could also provide solutions to the transport of goods. As Mikael Colville-Andersen explains, "Copenhagenize deals primarily with urban mobility, so regarding the transport of goods, which is and remains a great necessity for our societies, we focus on what can be done in cities as opposed to the logistics of transporting goods around Europe. Removing large trucks from our cityscapes is paramount, and many cities are working towards this goal. This means creating depots away from urban centers and using smaller trucks for distribution. And why not use bicycles? Cargo bikes have been a regular feature on the streets of Copenhagen for more than 100 years and are excellent for small transport jobs. Even companies like IKEA make bicycles with trailers available for customers who prefer transporting their purchases home by bike." Urban traffic is responsible for 40 percent of CO_2 emissions. Since tripling the amount of cycling in Europe while concurrently reducing individual motorized trips would save 49.1 million tons of CO_2 or 5 percent of CO_2 emissions from traffic, how can other cities learn from Copenhagen?

"What has happened in Copenhagen can happen anywhere. It has a densely built-up old city center, but is surrounded by broad boulevards, motorways and urban sprawl, making it appear like many other cities. When I look around here in Copenhagen with traffic planners from abroad, they can quite easily envision their own city if they squint their eyes a bit. Indeed, we're seeing it happen all over the world. I work with cities in Europe and North America that are implementing the same kind of infrastructure and bicycle-friendly facilities. Thirty years of best practice in Copenhagen have really debunked all the myths and now, in a way, it's just a matter of copy and paste."

Go forth, say Heien and Colville-Andersen, and Copenhagenize!

Underlining the claim to being the capital of cycling, the city of Copenhagen launced a bicycle counter on May 1st, 2009, on the City Hall Square. It measures cyclists passing by on the street and displays two numbers: total so far today and total so far this year. Until mid-June the total number rose to more than 300,000. Another meter was placed in Nørrebrogade, which is supposed to be the busiest bicycle street in Denmark. It counted between 30,000 und 35,000 cyclists each day in summer and even in snow, the number went up to a respectable, 16,000 cylists a day.

Sarget & Co. is a London-based bike store, or rather work-shop, in which founder Rob Sarget "gently restores vintage racers at the most relaxing, aesthetic pace," as Mikael Colville-Andersen from Copenhagenized experienced and documented it. What seems to be a long-standing, well-established store was in fact only launched in 2008 when Sarget wanted a "lifestyle change." It seems as if he and his customers are very happy with that choice.

OVERTREDERS W

The Dutch designers Overtreders (Reinder Bakker & Hester van Dijk), Maartje Dros and Eric Klarenbeek designed the pixellated mosaic walls of a bicycle tunnel in Zaandam in collaboration with local residents. Windmills, multiculturalism, traditional green "Zaanse" wooden houses, nature, the harbor and the flat Dutch polders: These are some of the impressions that adorn the walls of the "Pixelpoort" bicycle tunnel in Zaandam, just outside Amsterdam. The tunnel is situated along the route that leads to the ferry connecting Amsterdam and Zaandam, used by commuters traveling by bicycle or scooter. Its colorful walls provide a bright respite from the dreary industrial terrain that surrounds the site. The project was shaped by three conditions established by the designers: the walls had to be graffiti-proof, there were to be images of some sort that represented the region, and local residents could be invited to contribute to the project. The community responded enthusiastically: more than 800 people participated, some residents submitting 20 different drawings each. The final mural, 280 m long, is composed of a collage of the most inspiring images, giving a colourful insight into the dreams and nightmares of the local Zaankanters (Zaan residents).

SCHINDELHAUER BIKES Schindelhauer Bikes is a German brand from Magdeburg. Its bikes are designed to meet the challenges of daily commuting without compromising on style. The company's Gates Carbon Drive™ belt is a zero maintenance, no-muss-no-fuss system. These photographs show a selection of Schindelhauer models.

PAPER BICYCLE

—

The Paper Bicycle is not made out of paper, it is infinitely more hardy than that. Mechanical engineer and silversmith Nick Lobnitz, already known for his Carry Freedom foldable city trailer system, designed this new, yet retro city bike. It seems to recall simpler times and simpler joys, a design built not for athletics, tricks, or fashion but for real people who need to get to real places. The Paper Bike features an enclosed chain, mudguards, puncture-proof tires, hidden gears, cables and brakes, a child seat, dynamo light options, and a chain cover that can be custom printed. The Paper Bicycle's cromo steel frame comes with a lifetime warranty in one and eight-speed versions.

MARTIN ANGELOU

—

Bulgarian architect Martin Angelov wonders if it is possible to achieve a completely new level of transportation with minimum resources. When he entered an international competition to create a transportation hub "the first crazy idea that came to my mind was to make flying bicycle-lanes," he says. With only a pencil sketch, the idea earned a spot among the finalists. The Kolelinia midair bike lanes consist of steel cables suspended above city streets at a maximum of 4.5 meters and over pedestrian zones at between 2.5 to 3 meters. Commuters' bike tires are slotted into a steel furrow up to 13 cm deep and anchored to the two horizontal steel cables, with a third safety cable strung at about saddle height. The butt of one handlebar is also clipped to this third cable. Riders are clipped into the cable system via a harness worn around the upper thighs and waist, and if anything goes wrong, they are belayed via a rope. The harness itself is off-the-shelf climbing gear but the rest of the safety device is Angelov's invention. The system is not intended to replace ordinary biking, only to relieve congested zones. "We are born to move and this makes us alive," insists Angelov. "Transport is not just transport, it has to be an experience. The quality of this process reflects directly on the quality of our life."

146

VANMOOF   Giving a contemporary shape to the classic Dutch bike is the idea behind Vanmoof, a young bike brand launched in the Netherlands in 2009. The single-speed bike is stripped down to the very basics. No wires no worries. Front and rear LED lights are solar powered. The Vanmoof is made to resist a rough urban life, all daily commutes, being locked to anything, and being constantly outside and often in the rain, for urban dwellers in the Netherlands and beyond.

YIKEBIKE "Freedom to park wherever I damn well yike," reads the YikeBike website. Christchurch-based designer Grant Ryan created this voluptuous folding electric bicycle from carbon composite. It can reach speeds of up to 20 km/h, has a range of 10 km, and takes just 30 minutes to recharge. At 9.8 kg, the Yike can be carried in a bag when cyclists reach their destination. These impressive specs, combined with rising oil prices, might even make you yike rush hour.

GRACE E-MOTORBIKES Sustainability will not be sustainable if it fails to move people in personal ways. We have to relate to it, we have to like it. An electric motorbike with the sleek look of a high-end mountain bike, Grace combines style and longevity, and was designed by German inventor and entrepreneur Michael Hecken in collaboration with bike producer Karl-Heinz Nicolai.

GOCYCLE The Gocycle combines on-demand electric power, portability and city-specific design in-novations for a minimal-effort, zero-emissions, low-cost commute. Developed and manufactured in the U.K. by Karbon Kinetics Limited, Gocycle is an award-winning bike that is specifically designed for the city and offers performance commuting at a lower cost than public transport.

UNCOMMON PROJECTS

—

The designers at this Brooklyn-based software and hardware "innovation studio" are passionate about emerging technologies, interactivity, and digital media. Above all, Uncommon Projects is interested in "the intersection of daily life, creativity, and microprocessors." Their convention-breaking projects, as the studio puts it, have been viewed, heard, held, installed, played, ridden, and browsed. Commissioned by Yahoo!, UP designer Josh McKible researched and developed 20 photo-taking bikes in 10 weeks. UP was also responsible for developing the technology to make the bikes work. The prototypes of the ybike (2008) were designed to operate both domestically and internationally, and were shipped to 12 locations including Tanzania, Denmark, Tokyo [the image we have was taken in Tokyo], Lebanon, and the U.K. When ridden, the bikes were set to automatically take photographs and upload them to Flickr every 60 seconds. Each photo is tagged with the bike's GPS location so that it can be viewed on an interactive map. The bikes are weatherproof, location-aware, internet-connected, solar-enabled, and can work for up to two weeks on a single charge. The research, fabrication files, and source code were then freely shared for anyone to use and modify.

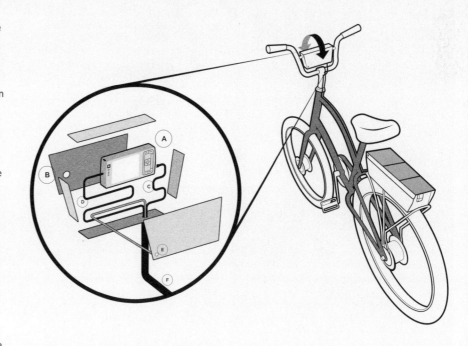

COPENHAGEN WHEEL

—

The Copenhagen Wheel is more than a wheel and is not entirely Danish. Handsome and responsive to its rider, the Copenhagen Wheel was designed by the SENSEable City Lab at Boston's Massachusetts Institute of Technology to keep pace with increasing urban mobility and connectivity. The high-tech wheel transforms ordinary bicycles into hybrid e-bikes that function as mobile sensing units, allowing riders to capture the energy expended while cycling and braking and save it

for when they need an extra push. It also maps pollution levels, traffic congestion, and road conditions in real-time. Using a smart phone, users can lock and unlock their bike, change gears, and select how much the motor assists them. As they cycle, the wheel's sensing unit captures their exertion levels and information about the surroundings, including carbon-monoxide, NOx and noise levels, ambient temperature, and relative humidity. Riders can access this data through their phone or

on the internet and use it to plan healthier bike routes, meet exercise goals, or catch up with friends. The data generated can also be shared with friends, or with the city — anonymously — to help build a fine-grained database of environmental information that is of benefit to everyone.

GOODMORNING
TECHNOLOGY
—

Copenhagen, one of the world's most
cycle-friendly cities, has now introduced the
CarGo — a colorful car-shaped parking shel-
ter for cargo bikes, designed by Goodmorning
Technology. The number of cargo bikes in
Copenhagen has increased dramatically in
recent years. Six percent of households in the
Danish capital now own at least one cargo
bike, which means that there are more than
15,000 in the city. But that's the way Copenhagen likes it: lots of bikes means fewer cars
and less pollution. However, the amount of
cargo bikes has resulted in an increased need
for parking solutions that secure the bikes
overnight and in bad weather — and that is
where the CarGo comes in.

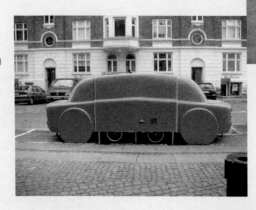

STUDIO TRACTOR Mark Kolodziejczak and Michael Tower of Brooklyn-based Studio Tractor joined forces with Peter Kirkiles of PKDF in 2009 to design the Cotter Pin bicycle rack for Connecticut's Aldrich Contemporary Art Museum. The piece evokes the simplicity of a bent metal cotter pin.

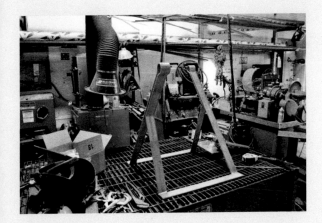

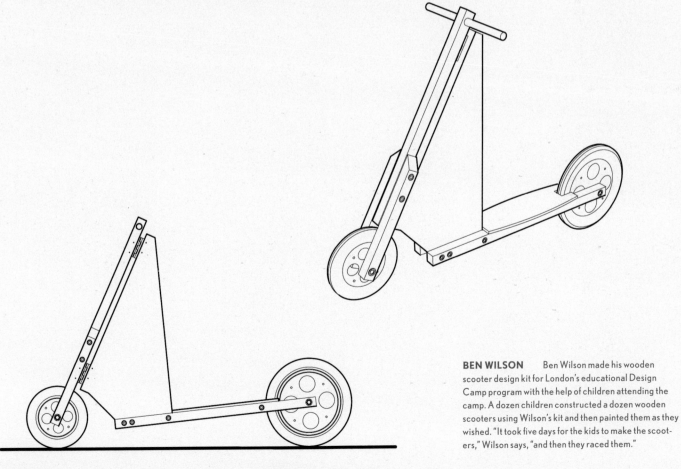

BEN WILSON Ben Wilson made his wooden scooter design kit for London's educational Design Camp program with the help of children attending the camp. A dozen children constructed a dozen wooden scooters using Wilson's kit and then painted them as they wished. "It took five days for the kids to make the scooters," Wilson says, "and then they raced them."

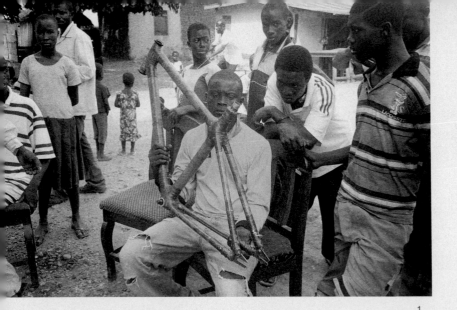

1

2

3

BAMBOO BIKE
STUDIO
—

The bicycle lovers at New Jersey-based
Bamboo Bike Studio teach people to build
bike frames out of bamboo, harvesting their
materials close to home. They have used their
engineering, teaching, and financial capital to
establish bamboo bike factories in developing
countries, starting with Ghana and Kenya.
—

1

Bamboo Bike Studio founder Marty Odlin traveled
to Ghana in the spring of 2009 in partnership with
Columbia University's Millennium Cities Initiative to
conduct research aimed at setting up bike factories in
this impoverished African country. Odlin gives villagers
a close-up look at the bamboo bike frames that could be
grown, harvested, and manufactured locally and sold for
a reasonable price.

2

The bicycle that BBS built for Ghana features a longer
wheelbase to better navigate the country's rugged terrain and manage local users' heavy cargo loads.

3

Marty Odlin and Sean Murray of Bamboo Bike Studio
harvesting bamboo in New Jersey. All the bamboo that
BBS uses for its bikes comes from the tri-state area.

4

A bamboo bike built by the Bamboo Bike Studio

4

1
PAPER BICYCLE   This DIY
bicycle trailer is designed by Nick
Lobnitz from Paper Bicycle. Instruc-
tions and plans can be ordered via
the Carry Freedom website. There
is no welding to be done, and no tube
bending. Make it yours, any size,
from any material, even bamboo.

2

2
TEUN VOETEN   Teun Voeten's portrait, taken in
Goma in the Democratic Republic of Congo, depicts a
young boy with a small chukudu. The chukudu, a wooden
scooter or bicycle used for transporting heavy loads, is
typical of the North Kivu Province. The name is derived
from the sound that the chukudu makes as it rolls along
the rocky local roads.

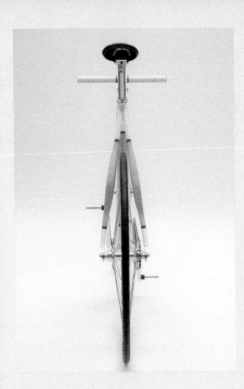

ARNDT MENKE   "Good morning. Check out this killer wooden bike," tweeted Lance Armstrong on Arndt Menke's 2008 Holzweg bike. Menke is a Berlin-based product designer who joined forces with Zumbragel to create a laminated pinewood bike. The Holzweg has the refined elegance of a real-tennis racket, a sleek carbon-fiber saddle, and a ribbon-like sculptured rear fork.

AURUMANIA

—

It is as if it was touched by Midas himself — Scandinavian design company Aurumania has made the most expensive golden bicycle in the world. Each bike in the numbered, limited-edition of 10 bears a price tag of €80,000 — no wonder, since each bike is hand-built, plated with 24-carat gold, and generously encrusted with more than 600 Swarovski crystals. The handlebar grips are hand-sewn from chocolate-brown leather and paired with an old-school Brooks molded leather saddle. The company has also designed other unusual bicycles: the first product in the CPH STREET range is the Night Bike, an intensely black single-speed street bike, conceived to meet the current fascination with track bikes — single-speed bikes with either no brakes or a single coaster brake. Aurumania designers intend it as a "state-ment of street chic" and "as an incredibly practical answer to urban mobility challenges."

DZINE

PUERTO RICAN ARTIST DZINE (CARLOS ROLON), WHO SPLITS HIS TIME BE-
TWEEN SAN JUAN AND CHICAGO, HAS TURNED LOWRIDER BIKES INTO
HIGH ART, MIXING A COCKTAIL OF POPULAR REFERENCES, BAROQUE
ROMANTICISM, CRAFTSMANSHIP, KALEIDOSCOPIC COLORS, AND INV-
ENTIVE APPROPRIATION.

1

His work makes a virtue of the overwhelming (rather than identity politics) and includes sculpture, large-scale paintings, installations, and hybrids that juxtapose studio paintings and video with his handmade "kustom kulture" bike and car sculptures. He has had solo shows at the Museum of Contemporary Art in Chicago and the Bass Museum in Miami, and has even created a custom artwork for Lance Armstrong. In 2007 at Art Basel Miami Beach, New York's Deitch Projects gallery held a Dzine exhibition called "Barrio Dreams." It featured work that was influenced by the Chicago lowrider bike culture, such as Lil' Dnipro, a customized lowrider tricycle wrapped in chrome and 24 carat gold leaf and with crystal-encrusted mirrors. The bike was accompanied by a 14 minute video and was created for the exhibition "A Poem About an Inland Sea," held in the Ukrainian Pavilion at the Venice Biennale — 52nd International Art Exhibition. Another of Dzine's lowrider bikes features custom-engraving, enamel, Bondo, steel, 24 carat gold plating, Swarovski crystals, and a mirror. Dzine's works are an apotheosis of the radio-fitted, radiantly decorated lowrider bikes seen on the summertime streets of Manhattan's Lower East Side, and they are now on display at some of the most revered museums and galleries in the world. Dzine is not making exuberant cultural statements, so much as an aesthetic one. Modification and customization, he suggests, are a step away from being fine works of art. Custom bike builders around the world, tinkering with a saddle shape or tweaking the angle of handlebars, will probably agree. Dzine's work is currently on show at a solo exhibition at the Bass Museum of Art, Miami. The opening was held during Art Basel in December 2009.
—

1
Ghost Bike (Detail), 2009. Custom lowrider tricycle with enamel paint, Swarovski crystals, mirror, fabric, video and audio.

2
Barrio Dreams, 2007. Custom lowrider bicycle 24 kt gold plating, chrome, enamel, Swarovski crystals, rubber and mirror. Image courtesy of the artist and Deitch Projects, New York.

3
Untitled (Custom lowrider bicycle), detail, 2008. Enamel, bondo, steel, 24kt gold plating, custom engraving, Swarovski crystals, and mirror.

2

3

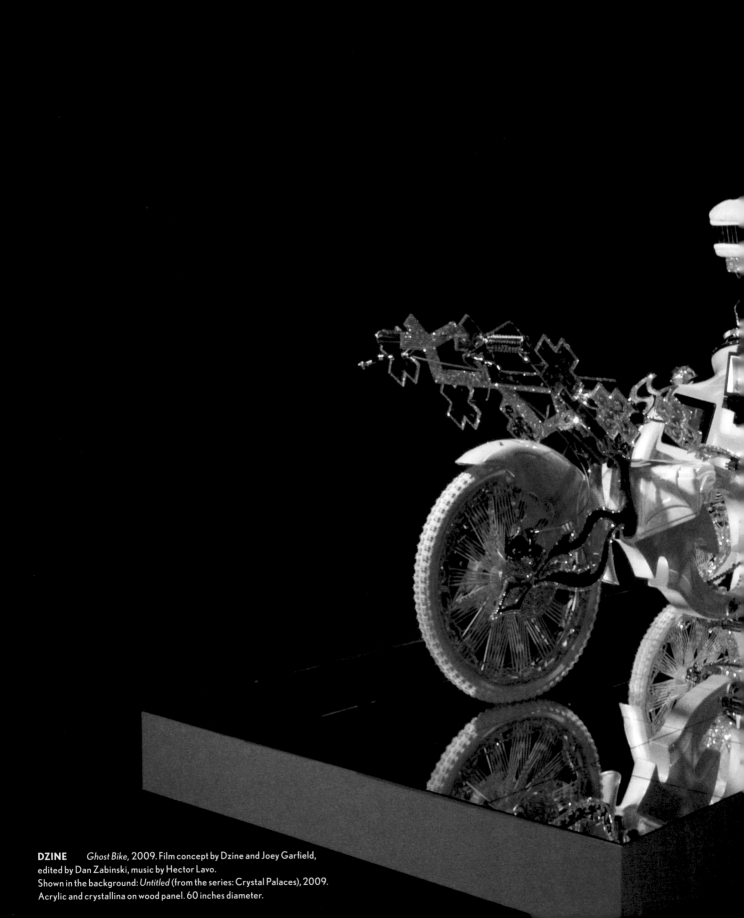

DZINE *Ghost Bike,* 2009. Film concept by Dzine and Joey Garfield,
edited by Dan Zabinski, music by Hector Lavo.
Shown in the background: *Untitled* (from the series: Crystal Palaces), 2009.
Acrylic and crystallina on wood panel. 60 inches diameter.

DZINE *Return of the Crown Prince (A carriage for Haile Selassie)*, 2009. Metal, oak, and cherry wood, 23 ct gold leaf, vintage boomboxes and speakers, car audio, electronics, mirror, velvet, rubber, and Swarovski crystals.

opposite page
Throne to the Last Emperor of the Forbidden City, 2008. Enamel paint, Swarovski crystals, custom engraving, 24 carat gold leaf, mirror, and fabric.

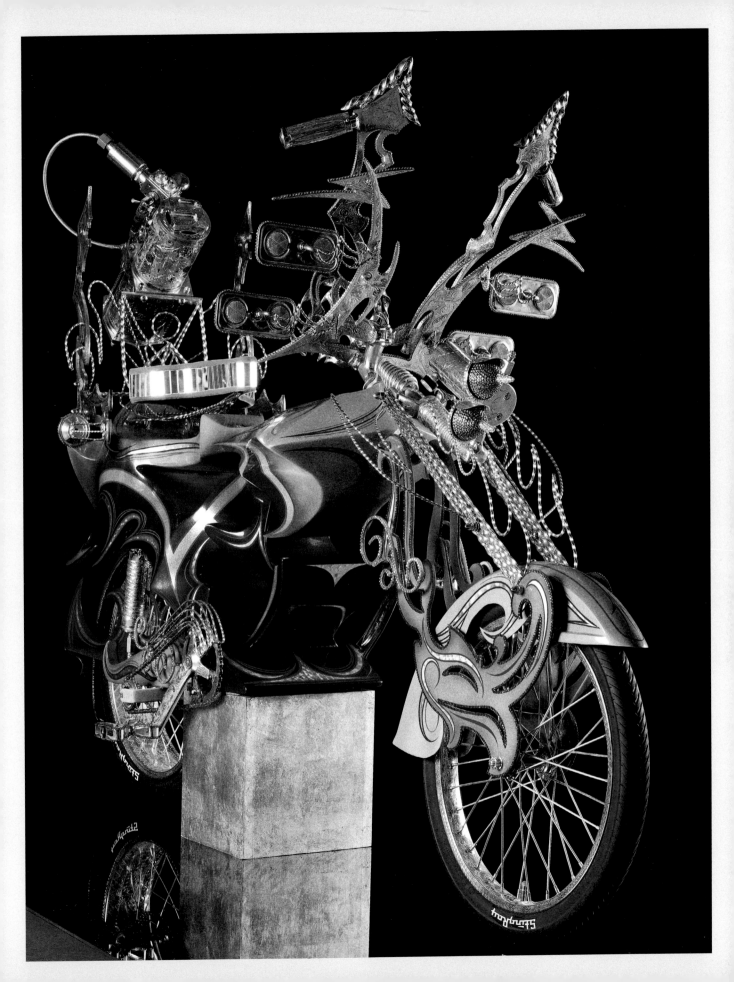

OLIVIER PASQUAL   Olivier Pasqual's photography studio is located in Geneva, Switzerland. He specializes in still-life photography for both the advertising industry and the fine art world. His shot this layout entitled *Superposition* for the magazine *the club VOICE*, n°35 / Swatch AG.

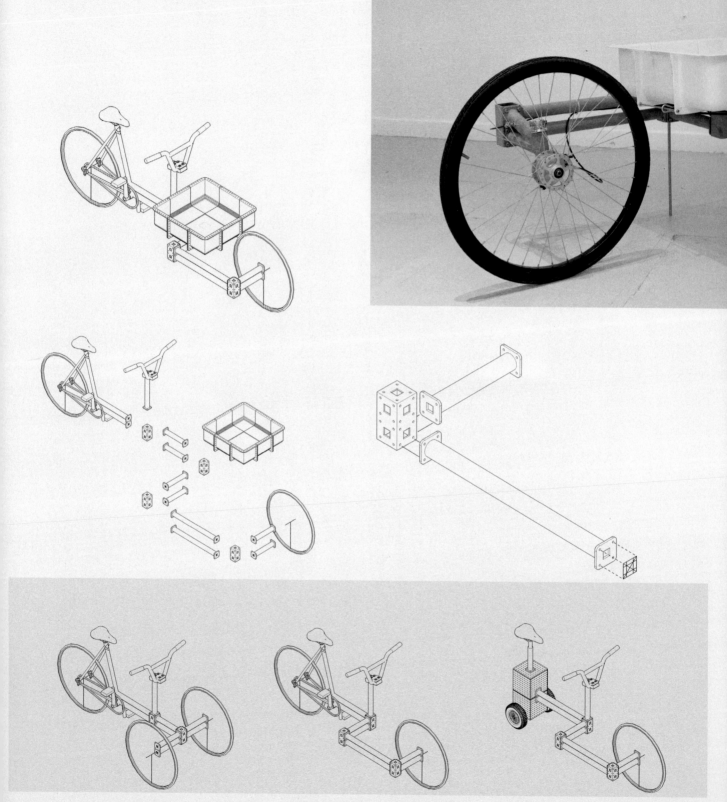

172

INTRASTRUCTURES
—

The OpenCargoBike prototype for OpenStructures features a mono-fork cable steering system and a duomatic gear box. Its Belgian designer, Jo van Bostraeten, describes the vehicle as "an open modulable design," which means, in part, that it is component-based and can be reconfigured according to the user's needs. The cargo bike can grow into a tandem, shrink into a city bike or be upgraded into an electrical bike simply by adding, subtracting, or replacing components. But the OCB is also an in-progress, open-source design and van Bostraeten invites anyone to contribute components of their own invention to help the CargoBike evolve into a better-adapted species over time. A common geometrical grid that is free of charge and shared by all participants forms the core of the OpenStructures concept, enabling designers to create compatible parts independently from one another. The ongoing development of the collaborative open-source bicycle could involve both individual cycling enthusiasts and major manufacturers.

MIGUEL LUCIANO   Brooklyn artist Miguel
Luciano's *Pimp my Piragua* (2008) is a mobile public art
project driven by pedal power that commemorates the
innovations of Latino street vendors by transforming a
traditional pushcart for selling shaved ice ("piraguas" in
Spanish) into "a hyper-modified pushcart tricycle" — with
a thumping hi-fi sound and video system.

1

NIHOLA BIKES   The 2001 Family model from German bike manufacturer Nihola features a rain hood and a bench for two children. The Dutch Association of Cyclists *(Fietsbond)* named Nihola the fastest and easiest steering transport bike. Seven thousand Nihola Family owners throughout Europe agree.

2

LARRY VS HARRY   Copenhagen-based Larry vs Harry are new to the bike scene, offering attractive and speedy cargo bikes — perfect for modern urban nomads who want to carry belongings with them wherever they go. Larry and Harry claim that, at 23 kilos, the 2009 Bullitt is the fastest cargo bike in the world.

1

2

4

The Family Tandem enables two or even three children to pedal along with their parents, up front where they learn to cycle.

5

The amazingly versatile and convenient Cargobike re-defined the "family bike" and spawned an ever-growing legion of imitations. Tens of thousands of Cargobikes are ridden by families and small businesses in the Nether-lands and elsewhere.

3

WORKCYCLES

1
A silent, safe, pollution-free, and convenient vehicle for street cleaning and trash collection. Trikes such as these have been used for decades by Dutch cities and park services.

2
The WorkCycles Fr8 is a modular transport bicycle that can be outfitted with carriers and accessories for many purposes, including carrying up to three children, deliveries and industrial internal transport.

3
These classic Dutch bikes *(bakfietsen)* have been in continuous production for almost 75 years. They drive at single-speed, have fixed wheel gearing, and are built for a variety of heavy-duty applications with a maximum load of 400 kg.

EMILIO SANTOYO

—

California-based illustrator and avid cyclist
Emilio Santoyo finds inspiration for many of
his illustrations in activities he observes on the
streets of Los Angeles and in the nearby city of
Rialto, where he lives and works. He invariably
has a series of projects on the go at the same
time: a weekly comic, magazine illustrations,
books, new products for his online store,
sketches for a new installation, or even, as he
puts it, "chasing down taco trucks."

—

The experience of going over his handlebars on his bike
was Santoyo's inspiration for *Over the bars and onto the
floor* (2008): "It is an experience that a person cannot
forget," he says.

178

Gimmie Gimmie (2008) was inspired by something that Santoyo observed on the streets of L.A.: a well-dressed couple were riding down the street, a large woman perched on the handlebars facing her boyfriend as he pedaled. "In times of economic struggle people have to cut some corners," Santoyo says.

BENJI WAGNER

EDITORIAL PHOTOGRAPHER BENJI WAGNER LIVES WITH HIS WIFE AND THREE SMALL CHILDREN IN PORTLAND, OREGON, A TOWN THAT IS HOME TO A BIKE FESTIVAL THAT INVERTS THE FUZZY OUTLINES OF THE GERMAN OKTOBERFEST – THE OREGON MANIFEST. IT CELEBRATES BOTH THE ARTISANAL ELEMENTS OF THE LOCAL BIKE SCENE AND BLIND PILOT, A BAND WHO HAVE MADE THEIR NAME AS MUCH FOR TOURING ON TWO WHEELS AS FOR THEIR MUSIC.

[1] Wagner has recorded the growth of the young craft movement of bicycle frame builders in the U.S. in general and in his own hometown in particular. His photographs capture both the technical dedication to, and the rich aesthetics of, making a human-powered machine. In rich color and black and white, Wagner documents these frame builders – Ira Ryan, Jordan Hufnagel, Matt Cardinal, Aaron Hayes, and Nate Meschke – as master tinkerers, inventors in equipment-littered labs. He has made portraits of many of the nearly 20 handmade bike builders that have sprouted up in Portland in recent years and who now make it not just one of the most bicycle-friendly cities in the U.S., but also one of the most beautifully crafted bicycle environments in the world.

—

[1]
Matt works on a custom fork in the Signal Cycles workshop.

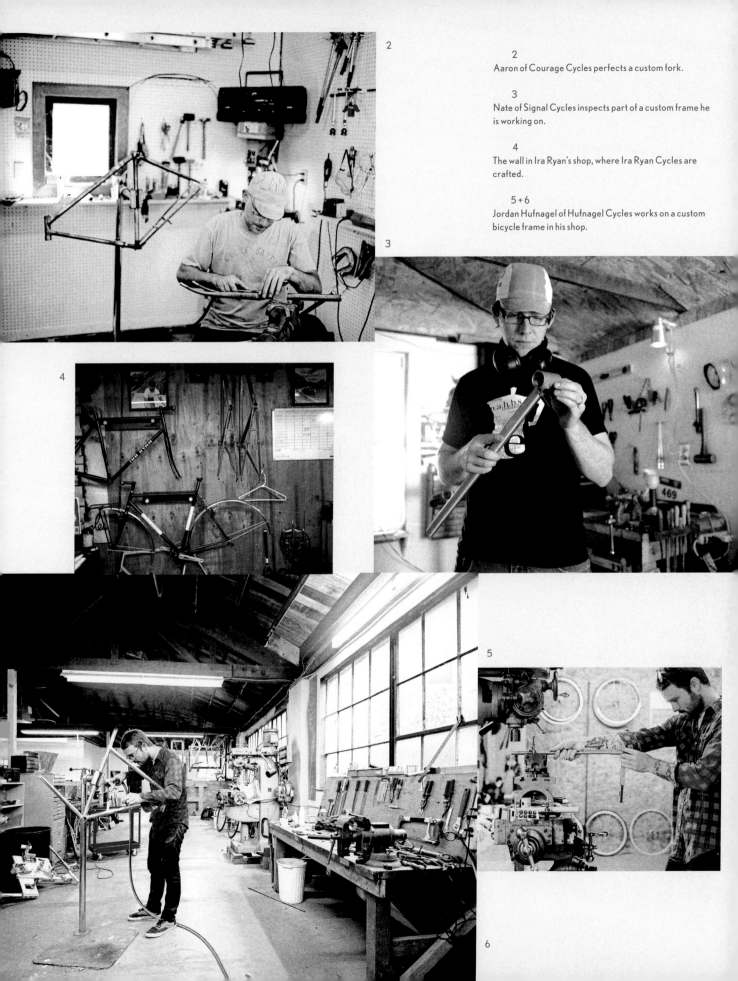

2
Aaron of Courage Cycles perfects a custom fork.

3
Nate of Signal Cycles inspects part of a custom frame he is working on.

4
The wall in Ira Ryan's shop, where Ira Ryan Cycles are crafted.

5 + 6
Jordan Hufnagel of Hufnagel Cycles works on a custom bicycle frame in his shop.

02 SPORTS MARKET-ING – THE "NORTH AMERICAN HANDMADE BICYCLE SHOW"

—

Taking place in a different U.S. city each year, the "North American Handmade Bicycle Show" exhibits the work of international bicycle artisans.

—

1

Master bike builder Richard Sachs, whose workshop is situated in Connecticut.

2

Jason Montano of Oakland manufacturer, Broakland.

3

Oregon-based Jordan Hufnagel introduces his touring bicycle at the 2009 "North American Handmade Bicycle Show."

1

2

3

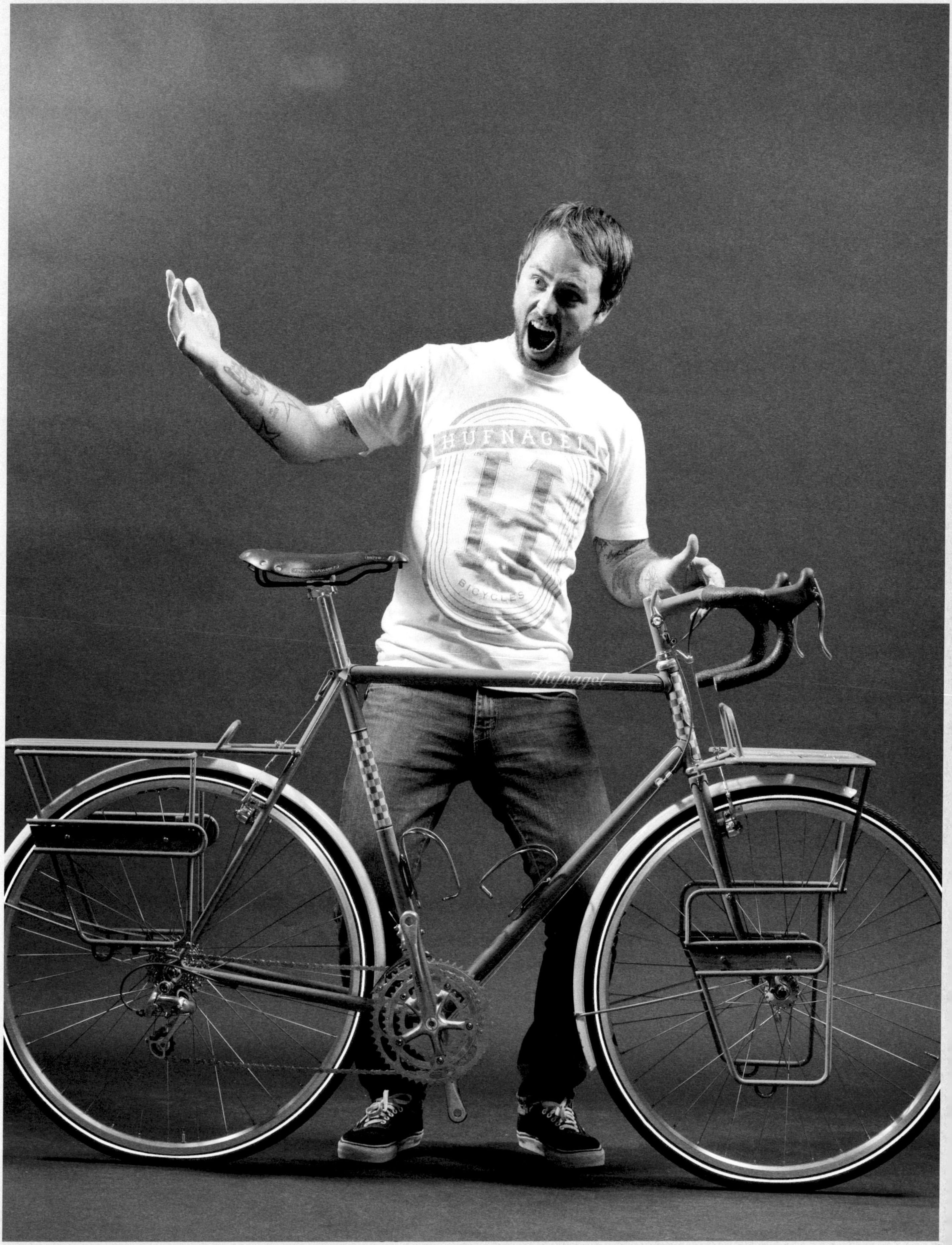

BIKE-OPOLIS

The battle over which North American city is the best for biking is fierce and—most likely—unresolveable. We can tell you which cities' residents make the largest percentage of their commutes by bike.

Portland, Oregon, you can keep on gloating.

NEW YORK: 0.7%
CHICAGO: 1.1%
WASHINGTON, D.C.: 1.7%
TORONTO: 1.7%
SAN FRANCISCO: 2.5%
VANCOUVER: 3.0%
MINNEAPOLIS: 3.8%
PORTLAND, OR: 3.9%

#8
#7
#6
#5
#4
#3
#2
#1

A COLLABORATION BETWEEN
GOOD AND CHRIS KORBEY

SOURCE: "Cycling and Walking for All New Yorkers: Path to Improved Public Health," by Professor John Pucher, Rutgers University

BIKE BY REPUBLIC BIKES:
www.republicbike.com

CHRIS KORBEY Equal parts designer, writer, and photographer, Dallas-based Korbey has worked in nearly every media for clients such as T-Mobile, General Mills, and the American Institute of Graphic Art. For *GOOD* magazine he made this information graphic, entitled *America's Most Bike-Friendly Cities*.

DEATH SPRAY CUSTOM   "Ride it, hold it, hit it, wear it, love it." The mantra of London's Death Spray Custom is all about functional vanity. DSC's Love/Hate handlebars were born of a love for both tattoos and cycling, and represent a tongue-in-cheek riposte to the occasional earnestness of the fixed-gear scene. A shade of baby-blue was combined with nail varnish and the iconic love/hate knuckle tattoo to create a product that toys with the conventions of style in a style-conscious community.

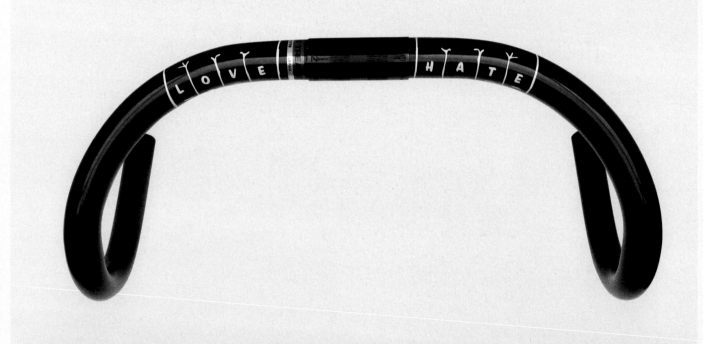

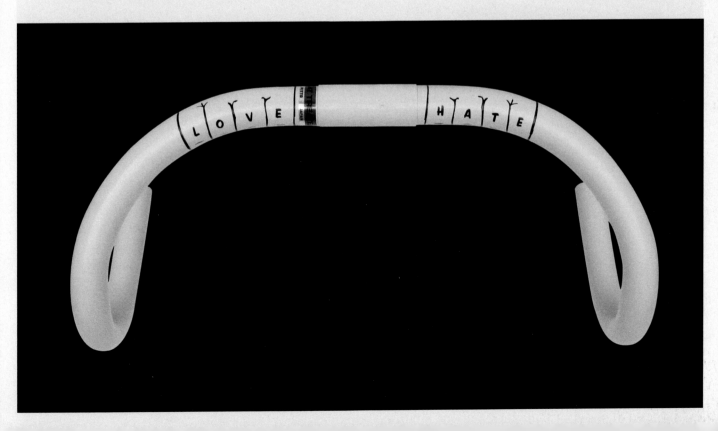

KEIKO NIWA   Still-life commercial and portrait photographer Keiko Niwa grew up in New York in a family of photographers. Her Brooklyn project "Bike Photo Booth", created for New York Bike Jumble in 2009, gave New York City cyclists the opportunity to get free professional portraits taken of themselves with their bikes.

AESTHETIC APPARATUS   When Minneapolis designers Dan Ibarra and Michael Byzewski established Aesthetic Apparatus in 1999, they just saw it as a hobby. But when their limited-edition screen-printed concert posters gained recognition and began winning awards, they finally gave up their day jobs. *Self-Portrait of a Bike Commuter* was their submission to the bike poster show, "ARTCRANK Minneapolis 2009."

LET'S RIDE!

1

2

1
GEMMA CORRELL   Gemma Correll is a U.K.
illustrator whose work often features a sweet naïveté,
humor, and small, chubby animals.
— Tote bag illustration.

2
JACQUELINE CZARNECKI   Virginia-based
designer and illustrator Jacqueline Czarnecki produced
this illustration for a promotional bookmark.

FRANCESCO BERTELLI

—

New York-based custom track bicycle builder Francesco Bertelli likes lugged steel, skinny tubes, quill stems, vintage cranksets, track geometry, leather and wood, unusual handlebars, and chrome forks. Buyers will find all these elements in his one-off *bici*. He does not like visible logos and stickers, threadless forks, clamp stems, visible welds, sponge grips, fake leather saddles, machined rims, or flip-flop wheels. Buyers will not find these on any of Bertelli's track, fixed-gear and coaster-brake bikes. He assembles, finishes, and fine-tunes every part by hand, combining brand-new parts with "new old stock" and vintage parts sourced from flea markets, old bike shops, collectors, and suppliers with whom he has developed long-standing relationships.

—

1
Domenica (2009).

2
Performa Brakeless (2009).

3
Domenica Sport (2009).

1

1
SEVEN CYCLES   Massachusetts' Seven Cycles, makers of the Viridian Bike, is the largest custom-bike manufacturer in the world and one of the most innovative designers of titanium frames. Seven Cycles uses customized frame geometry and rider-specific tube diameters and wall thicknesses to create bikes tailored to the cyclist's weight, riding style, intended use, age, and riding terrain. The company uses titanium, a metal alloy borrowed from the aerospace industry, for its ultra-light, super-strong, high-fatigue endurance, and corrosion-proof properties. Although Seven Cylces regularly designs bicycles for world-class athletes, president Rob Vandermark has also created the first titanium performance wheelchair.

2

BEN WILSON

—

Ben Wilson is a 3D industrial designer based in east London. He works with mass-produced products and on one-off handmade commissions. Oscar is a graphic designer working mainly in 2D, while Luke makes music. Occasionally, the three work together.

—

2

As part of the 2007 *AF1 Silver Service* installation at Dover Street Market, the Wilson brothers teamed up to create the AF1 Bike, a bespoke, traditionally lugged, steel-framed, hand-crafted, fixed-wheel bicycle. The design was finished off with white-on-white leather graphics and was included in an exhibition celebrating 25 years of the iconic Air Force 1 sneaker.

1

PARLEE CYCLES   Boston-based bike designer Bob Parlee gave his name to the Parlee Z1 in 2009. Because every human being is different, it seems only fitting that each bicycle should be custom-made. Parlee makes his carbon bikes from scratch and has been rewarded for his passion: the Z1 was the first carbon bike to be named *Bicycling Magazine* Editor's Choice for Dream Road Bike.

2

RICHARD SACHS   Longtime bike racer and master custom framebuilder, Richard Sachs learned his craft at London's Witcomb Lightweight Cycles. Twenty-five years later, Sachs crafted the Jokee, a series of steam-powered bikes, for Japanese manufacturer Shukuno-Rintendo. In 2007, he designed the AtmoSawa for his studio's permanent collection. It has been displayed twice at the "North American Handmade Bicycle Show" and has featured in one museum exhibition and in two books.

2

FENDI + ABICI

—

Fatto a Mano: The accessories adorning the Amante bicycle represent the consolidation of Fendi values and its alliance with bicycle manufacturer Abici. Fendi craftsmen turned out a refined goat-leather bag, a cover for a GPS navigator, a key and chain case, and a pump and thermos cover. Every feature for the Amante was cut, sewn, assembled, and embroidered by hand. A trunk, fully accessorized inside, replaces the common bike basket and resembles a luxury beauty case. The Fendi-styled bicycle draws on the company's rich tradition, the mastery of its Roman leatherworkers, and Abici's modern-day features.

CYCLE WORKS   The Cycle Works Company creates its sporty, working bicycles in the pure French Constructeur method. Cycle Works Oregon and Beloved are the result.

198

FREEMAN TRANSPORT Montana-based Free-man Transport was born out of the frustration of Ben Ferencz and Nathan Freeman with shipping of their bicycles. To solve the issue, their hand-made bikes use S-and-S couplings and can be easily disassembled and packed into an airline-approved bag with no oversized baggage fee.

1

1

AIRNIMAL   Based in Cambridge, U.K., Airnimal
was founded ten years ago by cyclists who wanted to be
able to transport their bikes easily, whether by car, train,
coach, or plane. It produces high-performance folding
bikes — this model was built to promote the 40th anniversary of the fashion label, Ben Sherman.

2

DIATECH PRODUCTS   Kyoto's Raw Design.Lab
created this small-wheel bike, the BRUNO VENTURA
STD, to evoke a road bike.

2

BROMPTON BICYCLE LTD. Scenes from the Brompton Factory in Brentford, U.K., where the company builds its folding bikes. The design of these modular frames has not changed since Andrew Ritchie filed the patent in 1979. Forty years later Ritchie won the Prince Philip Designers Prize for his work.

BIOMEGA
—

Copenhagen-based Biomega aims to create a paradigm shift in the way society views transportation. To this end, it wants to compete directly with cars by constructing bikes so stylish that they imbue cities with a new richness as they make riders (and those who breathe the air) healthier. The company draws on the expertise of some of the world's most celebrated product designers to create its models, with the result that Biomega bikes have been displayed in some of the most prestigious design museums around the world, including the Pompidou Centre in Paris, the Neues Museum in Munich, and the San Francisco Museum of Modern Art.
—

1
Biomega revisits the folding bike with this innovative show piece. If a thief cuts the integrated wire lock, the bike becomes unrideable … but once retrieved, it can be repaired.

2
Biomega's longest running success is the Copenhagen — a pared-down, quintessential gentleman's city bike. The Copenhagen Lady is just as minimal, urban, and sporty as the Copenhagen.

3
With its superplastic aluminium frame, Marc Newson's Biomega design offers an aggressive urban ride with integrated features and anti-corrosive properties.

1

2

3

MATT W. MOORE / MWM GRAPHICS

1
Series of five spray-painted track bike frames at the "Momentum" exhibition.

2
Exterior mural at the "Momentum" exhibition.

opposite page
Series of three posters by graphic designer Matt W. Moore from Portland, Maine. Shown in the "Momentum" exhibition at Open Bicycle in Somerville, Massachusetts in August 2009.

1

2

CINELLI
—

Italian racing pro Cino Cinelli founded his eponymous bicycle manu-
factory in 1948, drawing on 15 years of experience racing over every
imaginable type of road surface. Cinelli gave the cycling world the
modern handlebar, the first saddle to feature a plastic frame, the first
foot clips, and the first quick-release pedals. Thirty years later Cino
handed the company over to a young steel-tube industry entrepreneur,
Antonio Colombo, who sees the bike as a gesamtkunstwerk. Under
him, the Laser was born, lugs were abandoned, and TIG welding was
introduced as a way of improving the frame. Cinelli became the only
Italian bicycle to win a Compasso d'Oro in 1991. Competition is in the
Cinelli DNA and this has helped it to achieve many firsts in the industry:
the Rampichino (1985) introduced the MTB to Italy, Cork Ribbon
(1987) reinvented the bicycle ribbon, and Spinaci handlebar exten-
sions (1996) are used by over 800,000 cyclists today. The factory is
situated east of Milan.

—
1
The Gazzetta frame (2009) was designed by Alessandra
Cusatelli and has a minimal, striking steel track frame. A
micro-welded TIG junction and solid Columbus cromoly
tubes guarantee the strength and reliability of the frame
in any conditions. Unique to its market, the Gazzetta is
equipped with a traditional MTB-style segmented fork
(but with a track-correct 32 mm rake) and is intended
for use by the speedy and demanding urban or amateur
track cyclist. The Gazzetta comes in an exuberant
selection of "neo-pop" colors that complement the
minimal frame and leave it open to a myriad of art-tech
customizations.

2
The RVCA SuperCorsa Pista was produced in a limited
edition of 50. Its design was a collaboration between
Cinelli and renowned San Francisco artist Barry
McGee.

1

2

PAUL SMITH Paul Smith and Mercian Cycles

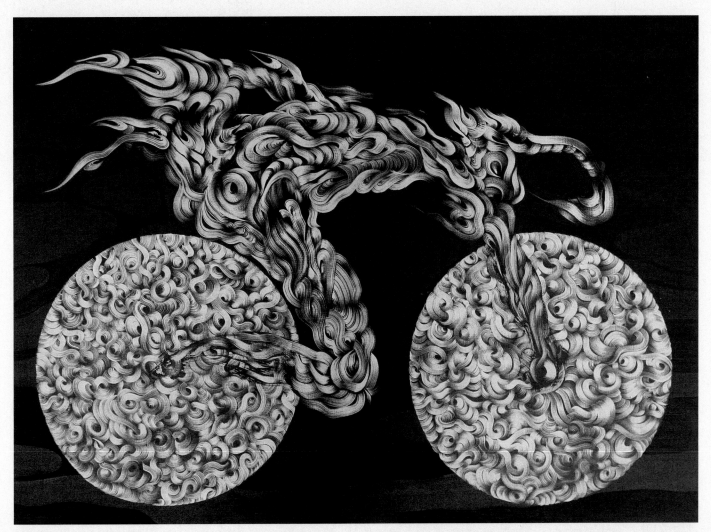

KOSUKE MASUDA Untitled painted on canvas (2009).

STEUIE GEE
—

Working as a graphic designer and art director by day and an illustrator by night, Stevie Gee admits that he "loves riding his bike hard and wild." Gee produced work for the "Vengeance is Coming!" exhibition in London.
—

1
El Capitane bike detail. "Vengeance is coming!" (2009).

2
Illustration for a bike built by Tourdeville and painted by Death Spray Custom for Jaguar Shoes.

1

2

3

4

5

3

Screen-printed felt flags designed by Gee, sewn by Sarah Parker, and printed by Stu:lovenskate.com for "Vengeance is Coming!"

4

Figo Vengeance bike detail, "Vengeance is Coming!" (2009).

5

The show included an exclusive fixed-bicycle collaboration with Tourdeville classic bike shop and Death Spray Custom. Detail depicts drowning men and doomed sailors.

6

While Stevie Gee was working in a San Francisco boxing gym in 2007, he met an old sailor called "El Capitane." El Capitane told Stevie an incredible story about a long-forgotten bike race that took place along the west coast of America in 1957. Sixty-six people started the race but only a Sioux medicine man, known as "Figo Vengeance," and El Capitane actually crossed the finish line.

6

CHAIRMAN TING   Canadian artist Carson Ting is the founder and creative director of this illustration studio. He created a time-lapse video of himself painting a wall in his Vancouver apartment. Shot with a tripod-mounted camera, the movie was assembled from 1,800 shots using only QuickTime Pro and iMovie. Because the mural incorporates an actual bike, Ting has a dedicated parking space for his wheels inside the apartment. If you love your bike enough, you won't want to leave it on the street. Ting's solution turns his bike into a piece of mobile furniture.

2

CANTGOSLO   This blogshop, based in Manchester, U.K., is as dedicated to selling biking apparel as it is to the culture of fixed-gear racing. The company borrows resourcefully from the iconic Milton Glaser "I Love NY" design, and its T-shirts play on "LOVE" being an anagram of "VELO."

2

JAY RYAN
—

Jay Ryan is an artist and musician from Chicago He started screen-printing in 1995, making posters and artworks for his own band (Dianogah) and his friends' bands. In 1999 he started the Bird Machine print shop where he produces limited run, hand-printed posters for bands and concerts, and for events such as art shows.

Jay Ryan's *not coming back* is produced by The Bird Machine, Inc. in Chicago, 2009.

FLABBYHEAD   *Tour de Force*, 2010.

Dancing even on the top
Bicycling at high gear
Final sprint at the finish
Flat tire on the paving stones

Last stage Champs-Elysees
Galibier and Tourmalet

Tour De France, Tour De France

Comrades and friendship

The peloton is regrouped

The bicycle is repaired quickly

INES BRUNN

YOU WONDER IF SHE IS GOING TO DANCE A TANGO, WALK A HIGH-WIRE, OR DO SOME FLIPS. AS IT TURNS OUT, INES BRUNN DOES ALL THREE — ON A MOVING BICYCLE.

Whether she is wearing lycra, sequins, or a beat-up pair of jeans, the 34-year-old artistic cyclist uses every foot and hand-hold she can find on a fixed-gear bike to power her way through routines that gymnasts usually do on a sprung floor. Brunn was the first woman to do a handstand on the handlebars of a bicycle.

Born in Germany, Brunn became a gymnast at the age of six, competing for seven years until she discovered artistic cycling, which she describes as "gymnastics on a bike." Within three years she had earned a place on the German national

The "Kunst Rad Show" has traveled through Asia, the U.S., and Europe, with Dunn performing up to 60 performances in a single month. Her tricks include extreme back-wheel riding and spinning, wheelies, handstands, planche push-ups, 360-degree flips around the handlebars, and headstands on the saddle. Brunn performs on torn-up city streets as often as on smooth indoor stages.

"The queen of fixed gear" performs on an original trick bike with a 1:1 gear ratio and sometimes on a unicycle. She also rides a small track bike that has a 45-tooth chain ring, an 18-tooth

cog, and a smaller front wheel to allow her to bar spin. Dunn's collection also features a blue Corima track-style fixed-gear bike with a front brake, a pink Cinelli, and a 1970s Chinese Flying Pigeon light roadster that she restored herself.

When Brunn moved to Beijing, she discovered that the Chinese, who are traditionally known for traveling by pedal-power, now register more than 1,800 new cars each day and often park them blocking bike lanes. In 2007, Brunn founded the Beijing Fixed Gear Bike Group, which grew from seven members to 70 within the first year. By 2008, she had quit her day job at a telecommunications company to open a fixed-gear bike shop. "We tend to focus on modern technologies and forget about solutions that prevailed for centuries," Brunn pointed out during a lecture she gave at TEDxBeijing 2009. "This was not because of a lack of innovation; it was due to the ingenious simplicity of the solution — like the bicycle."

—

team. Today, after competing for 16 years (and earning a degree in physics), Brunn performs seven-minute routines choreographed to music, as if dancing intimately with a long-time partner with whom she is perfectly in synch (and in love).

1
Ines Brunn doing her signature bicycle trick called "Ines Straddle" at the Hansa Variety Theater in Hamburg.

Doing a free-handed wheelie in Beijing, 2009.

1
Tricks on a tall bike at night in Orlando, 2008.

2
Ines Brunn appeared on the German TV show, *Wetten, das*, and bet that she could make a pancake standing on her bike. She succeeded.

3
Trick bike pirouette.

4
Doing the handstand during her trick bike show. Ines was the first female junior to do a handstand on a bike.

opposite page
Bike tricks at the TEDxBeijing conference.

2

3

4

1

2

2
EMILIO SANTOYO   *Bike Parade* (2007) depicts
one of the midnight rides in Los Angeles in which Santoyo
participates. "It's a great thing to be a part of," the designer
says. "The ride is full of different kinds of people riding different kind of bikes. You feel very welcome as people come
out of bars, houses, and maybe work to yell and cheer you on
as you ride by."

BRICOLEURBANISM
—
Toronto-based urban designer Robin Chubb is blogging from Shanghai. He produces an ongoing series of photographs that represent "reflections on the city, the landscape, and the fields that manipulate them" from the perspective of urban design, of landscape architecture, and from a Canadian-born photographer. Chubb has documented the myriad incidental ways that bicycles move the metropolis.
—
A balloon-seller at Longcao Road and Caodong Branch Road, Shanghai.

Transporting empty styrofoam containers from a wet market
on Tiayuan Road and Jianguo Rd, Shanghai.

Moving furniture by bicycle beside half-demolished build-
ings along Wanping South Road, Shanghai.

Transporting potted plants by bicycle along Caodong
Branch Road, Shanghai.

A tricycle stacked with cardboard for recycling on
Tianyaoqiao Road, Xujiahui, Shanghai.

A

ADAM TICKLE
www.thingsiveseen.co.uk

Raleigh Vector, 2007.
Photographer: Adam Tickle and others
Page 96

Bike Lock Up, 2010.
Designer: East London Bike Community
Photographer: Adam Tickle / Things I've Seen
Pages 94 – 95
—

AEOLIAN RIDE
www.aeolian-ride.info
www.sonicribbon.com
www.jessicafindley.com

Aeolian Ride, 2009.
Photographer: Jessica Findley
Pages 80 – 83
—

AESTHETIC APPARATUS
www.aestheticapparatus.com

Self-Portrait of a Bike Commuter, 2009.
Client: "ARTCRANK Bike Print Show"
Manufacturer: Screen-printed at Aesthetic Apparatus
Page 190
—

AIRNIMAL
www.airnimal.eu

2005.
Photographer: Richard and Anne Lewis
Page 201
—

ALLAN YOUNG
stuffmadefromstuff.net

Stuff made from stuff, 2009.
Page 134
—

ARNDT MENKE
www.arndtmenke.de

Holzweg, 2008.
Photographer: Andreas Velten,
Arndt Menke-Zumbrägel
Pages 160 – 161
—

AURUMANIA
www.aurumania.com

Aurumania, 2008.
Photographer: Aurumania
Pages 162 – 163
—

B

BAMBOO BIKE STUDIO
www.bamboobikestudio.com

Bamboo Bike Studio, 2009.

[1]
Photographer: Marty Odlin

[2, 3, 4]
Photographer: Joe Zorilla
Page 158
—

BEN WILSON
www.wilsonbrothers.co.uk
www.benwilsondesign.co.uk

Seebikesaw, 2009.
Photographer: Matthew Naylor
Client: Brooks England
Manufacturer: Ben Wilson Design
Page 68

Walk The Plank, 2009.
Photographer: Dan Canyon
Client: Walk The Plank / Arts Council England
Pages 88 – 89

Wooden Scooter, 2009.
Photographer: Ben Wilson
Client: Design Camp
Manufacturer: Ben Wilson Design / Kids on camp
Pages 156 – 157

Fixed-wheel bicycle, 2007.
Designer: Ben Wilson / Oscar Wilson / Wilson Brothers
Client: Nike
Photographer: Alexis Chabala
Page 194
—

BENJI WAGNER
www.benjiwagner.com

Various photos, 2009.
Page 180 – 181
—

BIG KID BIKE
www.bigkidbike.com

[1, 2]
The Kitten, 2008.
Designer: Greg deGouveia
Photographer: Greg deGouveia
Manufacturer: bigkidbike.com

Bigger Wheel 3, 2003.
Designer: Greg deGouveia
Photographer: Greg deGouveia
Manufacturer: bigkidbike.com
Page 63

[1]
Bigger Wheel 4, 2004.
Designer: Greg deGouveia
Photographer: Greg deGouveia
Manufacturer: bigkidbike.com

[2]
Jesus Lizard, 2006.
Designer: Greg deGouveia
Photographer: Greg deGouveia
Manufacturer: bigkidbike.com
Page 64

[3]
Bigger Wheel 5, 2005.
Designer: Greg deGouveia
Photographer: Greg deGouveia
Manufacturer: bigkidbike.com

[4]
Bigger Wheel 1, 2003.
Designer: Greg deGouveia
Photographer: Greg deGouveia
Manufacturer: bigkidbike.com
Page 65
—

BIOMEGA
www.biomega.dk

Puma Disko, 2009.
Designer: KibiSi
Photographer: Søren Nellemann, www.facefoto.dk

[2]
Copenhagen and *Copenhagen Lady*.
Designer: Jens Martin Skibsted
Photographer: Søren Nellemann, www.facefoto.dk

[3]
MN Carbon.
Designer: Marc Newson
Pages 204 – 205
—

BRICOLEURBANISM
www.bricoleurbanism.org

Balloon seller, 2009.
Photographer: Robin Chubb
Pages 222 – 223

Styrofoam containers, 2009.
Photographer: Robin Chubb
Page 224

Moving furniture, 2009.
Photographer: Robin Chubb
Page 225

Potted plant, 2009.
Photographer: Robin Chubb
Page 226

Cardboard for recycling, 2009.
Photographer: Robin Chubb
Page 227
—

BROMPTON BICYCLE LTD
www.brompton.co.uk

Various, 2009.
Photographer: Gilles & Cecilie Studio and others
Pages 202 – 203
—

C

CANTGOSLO
www.cantgoslo.com

Velo, 2009.
Photographer: Cantgoslo
Page 212
—

CHAIRMAN TING
www.chairmanting.com

Chairman Ting Bicycle Wall Art, 2009.
Designer: Carson Ting
Client: Chairman Ting Industries
Photographer: Carson Ting
Page 212
—

CHERYL DUNN
www.cheryldunn.net

Bicycle Gangs of New York, 2003 + 2004.
Photographer: Cheryl Dunn
Pages 70 – 73
—

CHRIS GILMOUR
www.chrisgilmour.com

Photographer: Marco De Palma
Courtesy of Perugi artecontemporanea
Page 125
—

CHRIS KORBEY
www.chriskorbey.com
www.good.is/post/transparency-biking-to-work/

America's Most Bike-Friendly Cities, 2009.
Designer: Chris Korbey
Art Director: Morgan Clendaniel, Atley Kasky
Client: GOOD magazine
Photographer: Chris Korbey
Page 184
—

CHRISTINA OH
www.christinaoh.com

Untitled, 2008.
Photographer: Christina Oh
Page 124
—

CINELLI
www.cinelli.it

1
Gazzetta, 2009.
Designer: Alessandra Cusatelli
Photographer: Cinelli

2
Cinelli x RVCA Supercorsa Pista, 2008.
Designer: Barry McGee and Cinelli
Photographer: Pier Maulini
Page 208
—

COPENHAGEN WHEEL
www.senseable.mit.edu

The Copenhagen Wheel, 2009.
Photographer: maxtomasinelli.com
Pages 152 – 153
—

COPENHAGENIZE
www.copenhagenize.com

Pages 138 – 141
—

CYCLE WORKS
www.belovedcycles.com

CWO/Beloved Cycles (cycling cap), 2009.
Designer: weights&pulleys ltd.
Client: Cycle Works Oregon, Inc.
Manufacturer: Little Package
Photographer: Michael Jones
Page 115

CWO/Beloved Cycles.
Model: No Haste.
Model: Morton.
Model: There and Back.
Designer: weights&pulleys ltd.
Photographer: Michael Jones
Page 197

CWO/Beloved Cycles.
Model: Every Day, Morton, Half Full.
Designer: weights&pulleys ltd.
Photographer: Chris Milliman
Pages 198 – 199
—

CYCLOWNS
www.cyclown.org

Cyclown Circus in Gent, Belgium, 2009.
Photographer: Christine de Pierro
Subject: Drummer Janski Rascal
Page 26

1
Cyclown Circus in Jakarta, Indonesia, 2007.
Photographer: Piero Silvestro

2
Cyclown Circus in Indonesia, 2009.
Photographer: Christine de Pierro
Subject: Raffe Cataldo
Page 27

Cyclown Circus in Bruges, Belgium, 2008.
Photographer: Christine de Pierro
Page 28
—

D

DAN FUNDERBURGH
www.danfunderburgh.com

l'Alpe d'Huez Brooks Team Pro Saddle, 2009.
Manufacturer: Brooks England
Page 112

New Hope Assembly of God, 2008.
Printed by Polluted Eyebal Brooklyn
Page 114
—

DANE COLELLA
www.pengull.com

1
Flyer, 2009.
Photographer: Luke Elrath

2
Tweed Ride, 2009.
Photographer: Dane Colella
Subject: John Lattanzio

3
Tweed Ride, 2009.
Photographer: Dane Colella
Subject: Tyler Petrus
Page 22

4
Tweed Ride, 2009.
Photographer: Dane Colella
Subject: Gary Rothera
Page 23
—

DASHING TWEEDS
www.dashingtweeds.co.uk

2007.
Photographer: Guy Hills
Model: Iris Palmer
Pages 108 – 109
—

DEATH SPRAY CUSTOM
www.deathspraycustom.com

Love/Hate bars, 2009.
Photographer: David Gwyther
Page 185
—

DESIGN BY MUSIC
www.designbymusic.com

BMX, 2009.
Client: Grafik Magazine / London Design Festival 09
Manufacturer: Manchester BMX Club
Photographer: Tim Sinclair
Pages 120 – 121
—

DIATECH PRODUCTS
www.diatechproducts.com

BRUNO VENTURA STD, 2010.
Designer: Raw Design.Lab
Page 201
—

DZINE
www.dzinestudio.com

1
Ghost Bike, 2009.
Photographer: Mariano Costa Peuser
Courtesy of Yuz Foundation

2
Barrio Dreams, 2007.
Photographer: Andreas Larsson
Courtesy of the artist and Deitch Projects, New York

3
Untitled (Custom Lowrider Bicycle), 2008.
Photographer: Andreas Larsson
Courtesy of Emily Murphy Art, Madrid
Page 164–165

Ghost Bike, 2009.

Shown in the background
Untitled (from the series: Crystal Palaces).
Photographer: Mariano Costa Peuser
Courtesy of Yuz Foundation
Page 166–167

Return of the Crown Prince (A carriage for Haile Selassie),
2009.
Photographer: Andreas Larsson
Courtesy of the artist and Deitch Projects, NY
Page 168

Throne to the Last Emperor of the Forbidden City, 2008.
Photographer: Andreas Larsson
Courtesy of The Steven and Alexandra
Cohen Collection
Page 169

Custom lowrider bicycle, 2009.
Photographer: Alex Lee
Courtesy of the Leeahn Gallery, South Korea.
Pages 238 – 239
—

E

EMCEE C.M.
www.emceecm.com

MOBILIZE: The Moving Picture Show, 2004.
Designer: Emcee C.M., Master of None

Frame: Worksman
Attachments: Emcee C.M., Master of None
Photographer: Carl Glassman
Page 87

1
Umbrella tarp for MOBILIZE street parking, 2004.
Photographer: Emcee C.M., Master of None
—

EMILIO SANTOYO
www.emiliospocket.com

Over the bars and onto the floor, 2008.
Page 178

Gimmie Gimmie, 2008.
Page 179

Bike Parade, 2007.
Page 220 – 221
—

ERIC STALLER + STALLERSTUDIO
www.conferencebike.com
www.ericstaller.com

Lovebike, 2008.
Photographer: Eric Staller
Client: Stallerstudio Netherlands
Manufacturer: Nijland Products

ConferenceBike, 1994,
Photographer: Jim McGurn
Get Cycling, York, England
Client: Stallerstudio Netherlands
Manufacturer: Velo Saliko
Page 69
—

F

FENDI + ABICI
www.fendi.com

Page 196
—

FIXIE SHIRT
www.fixie-shirt.com

*Fixie Shirt meets Pedal (Bike Messenger
Service, Brussels)*, 2009.
Page 85
—

FLABBYHEAD
www.flabbyhead.com

Tour de Force, 2009.
Pages 214 – 215
—

FOLDING WHEELS
www.folding-wheels.com

Foldable wheels, 2009.
Designer, photographer: Duncan Fitzsimons
Page 135
—

FORMPASCH
www.formpasch.com

PUYL, 2009.
Designer: Kai Malte Röver
Page 104
—

FRANCESCO BERTELLI
www.bertellibici.com

1
Domenica, 2009.
Manufacturer: Francesco Bertelli & Viking Cycles
Photographer: Francesco Bertelli

2
Performa Brakeless, 2009.
Manufacturer: Francesco Bertelli & Viking Cycles
Photographer: Francesco Bertelli

3
Domenica Sport, 2009.
Manufacturer: Francesco Bertelli & Viking Cycles
Photographer: Francesco Bertelli
Pages 192 – 193
—

FREEMAN TRANSPORT
www.freemantransport.com

Page 200
—

FRETSCHE
www.fretsche.ch

1
Original model Dolder Deluxe, 1978.
Photographer: Fretsche / Thomas Neeser
Client: Cilo

2
Selnau Deluxes, 2009.
Designer: Thomas Neeser
Photographer: Fretsche / Thomas Neeser

3
Albisrieden Sprint, 2009.
Designer: Thomas Neeser
Photographer: Fretsche / Thomas Neeser

4
Bubentraum, 2009.
Designer: Thomas Neeser
Photographer: Fretsche / Thomas Neeser

5
Dolder Deluxe, 2009.
Designer: Thomas Neeser
Photographer: Fretsche / Thomas Neeser

opposite page
Bubentraum, 2009.
Designer: Thomas Neeser
Photographer: Fretsche / Reto Jud
Pages 60 – 61
—

FROST PRODUKT
www.altabikes.no

Alta Bike.
Photographer: Pål Laukli
Manufacturer: ALTA Bike
Pages 12 – 13
—

G

GEMMA CORRELL
www.gemmacorrell.com

Let's Ride!, 2009.
Happiness This Way, 2009.
Page 191
—

GERHARD STOCHL
www.stochlfoto.com

Bike NY, Gerald Ding, 2008.
Photographer: Gerhard Stochl
Page 92

Bike NY, Dominic Neitz, 2008.
Photographer: Gerhard Stochl
Page 93

Bike NY, Dan Funderburgh, 2008.
Photographer: Gerhard Stochl
Page 93

Bike NY, Joel Barnard, 2008.
Photographer: Gerhard Stochl
Page 93

Bike NY, Daniel Piwowarczyk, 2008.
Photographer: Gerhard Stochl
Page 93
—

GOCYCLE
www.gocycle.com

Gocycle, 2009.
Designer: Richard Thorpe
Manufacturer: Karbon Kinetics Limited
Page 150
—

GOODMORNING TECHNOLOGY
www.gmtn.dk

Bikeporter, 2009.
Photographer: Goodmorning Technology
Client: Copenhagen Parts, copenhagenparts.com
Page 68

CarGo, 2009
Photographer: Goodmorning Technology
Client: Copenhagen City Council
Page 154
—

GRACE E-MOTORBIKES
www.grace.de

GRACE E-Motorbike, 2008.
Client: GRACE E-Motorbikes
Photographer: Christoph Martin
Page 149
—

GUU-WATANABE
www.guu-watanabe.com

Sakura.
Page 115

Various.
Photographer: Watanabe Tomoko
Pages 116 – 117
—

H

HOUSE INDUSTRIES
www.houseindustries.com

Photographer: 2009 Carlos Alejandro,
www.caphoto.com

[2]
Photographer: 2009 Anthony Skorochod

[3]
House Industries Wool Cycling Team Kit, 2009
Photographer: Carlos Alejandro

[4]
Velocipede, 2009
Photographer: Carlos Alejandro
Page 111
—

I

INDEPENDENT FABRICATION /
NACCC / TYLER EVANS
http://hurr.wentworthless.net

Various, 2009.
Photographer: Tyler Evans
Pages 6 – 9
—

INES BRUNN
www.natooke.com

Riding barefoot, 1997.
Ines Straddle, 1998.
Free-handed wheelie on track bike, 2009.
Photographer: Simon Lim
Track-bike surfing and umbrellas, 2009.
Photographer: Simon Lim
Pages 216 – 217
—

[1]
Tricks on Tall Bike, 2008.
Photographer: Udo Fetzer

[2]
Pancake bet on "Wetten, dass", 1998.

[3]
Trick-bike pirouette, 1999.

[4]
Handstand on bicycle, 1998.
Bike tricks at TED, 2009.
Photographer: Michele Travierso
Pages 218 – 219
—

INTRASTRUCTURES
www.keirin.be
www.openstructures.net

Open Cargo Bike, 2009.
Designer: Jo Van Bostraeten
Client: OpenStructures
Photographer: Kristof Vrancken
Linedrawings: Keirin / Intrastructures
Pages 172 – 173
—

J

J. ADELAIDE MÉTIVIER
http://shuttersquids.com

Bearded Madman, 2008.
Photographer: J. Adelaide Métivier
Cyclist: Dane Colella
Page 99
—

JRUITER + STUDIO
www.jruiter.com

Inner City Bike, 2009.
Client: jruiter + studio
Photographer: Jay Irwin, Mark Baas
Model: Alan Close
[below]
Photographer: Dean Van Dis
Page 66
—

JACQUELINE CZARNECKI
www.degreeslatitude.com

Book Bike, 2009.
Client: 2nd ed. Booksellers
Page 191
—

JASON KINNEY
www.jasonkinney.net

"ARTCRANK Portland," 2009.
Photographer: Jason Kinney
Pages 128 – 129
—

J – M

JAY RYAN
www.thebirdmachine.com

Not Coming Back, 2009.
Page 213
–

JNSNP (JAO-NOO-SINGH-NAK-PAN)
http://jnsnp.wordpress.com

JNSNP portrait, 2009.
Designer: Kachain Wonglamthong
Photographer: Kachain Wonglamthong
Pages 32 – 33

Hey!, 2009.
Designer: Mamafaka
Page 35

Man BMX, 2009.
Designer: BR&NDBOOK
Photograper: BR&NDBOOK
Page 76

Fucking Lane of Dead, 2009.
Designer: Oaky Jew
Page 90

Otaku Bike, 2009.
Designer: Rukkit Kuanhawate
Client: "Ride a Life"
Page 91

"Ride a Life," 2009.
Designer: TIKKYWOW
Page 127

Poster, "Ride a Life," 2009.
Designer: MAMAFAKA
Page 127

"Ride a Life" exhibition, 2009.
Page 127

"Life a Ride," 2009.
Designer: GoTToH x Shittak
Pages 220 – 221
–

JONATHAN BRAND
www.jonathanbrand.com

Fallen, 2007.
Photographer: Jonathan Brand
Page 124
–

JUD TURNER
www.judturner.com

BioCycle, 2008.
Abilicycle, 2009.
Photographer: Jud Turner
Page 123
–

K

KEIKO NIWA
www.keikoniwaphotography.com

Bike Photo Booth, 2009.
Client: NY Bike Jumble
Photographer: Keiko Niwa
Additional credits: Jeff Tancil and Harry Schwartzman
Pages 186 – 189
Artwork: Danielle Baskin, www.bellehelmets.com
Page 186
–

KEVIN CYR
www.kevincyr.net

Golden light shines above, 2008.
Page 46

In Beijing, China, 2008.
Photographer: Kevin Cyr
Page 47

Bear your motherland in mind while casting your eyes on the world, 2007.
Page 48

Camping far out in the wilderness forges a revolutionary heart, 2007.
Page 49
–

KOSUKE MASUDA
http://ko5.jp/

Cover art *Cover art for Volume #5 of COG magazine*.
Photographer: Peter DiAntoni
Client: *COG* magazine
Pages 58 – 59

Shimano Dura Kabuto.
Pages 96 – 97

Various, 2007.
Photography: Kei Hompo
Page 113

Untitled painted on canvas, 2009.
Page 209
–

L

LARRY VS HARRY
www.larryvsharry.com

Bullitt, 2009.
Photographer: Ole Nordmand
Page 175
–

LAURA CRAWFORD
www.tangerinetreehouse.com

The Bike Mustache, 2009.
Photographer: Russ Roca
Page 113
–

M

MARCO FACCIOLA

Wooden bike, 2008.
Photographer: Marco Facciola
Page 126
–

MARCO ZAMORA
www.marcozamora.com

Untitled, 2009.
Page 10

Making Moves 3, 2009.
Page 11

Product 1, 2009.
Page 78

Wild Life, 2007.
Page 79

Installation FIFTY24PDX, 2009.
Page 131
–

MARIE LOUISE GUSTAFSSON
www.marielouise.se

Bike basket Carrie, 2007.
Client: Design House Stockholm
Manufacturer: Design House Stockholm
Page 115
–

MARISA ABAZA
www.marisabaz.com

New York City cyclists, 2008.
Photographer: Marisa Abaza
Pages 38 – 41
–

MARK JENKINS
www.xmarkjenkinsx.com

Spokes, 2010.
Photographer: Mark Jenkins
Page 122
–

MARTIN ANGELOV
http://kolelinia.com

Kolelinia, 2010.
The Kolelinia project is under creative commons license
(cc) by-nc-nd
Page 146
—

MATT COLEMAN
www.mynameismattcoleman.com

The Water Cycle, 2008.
Page 136
—

MATT W. MOORE / MWM GRAPHICS
http://mwmgraphics.com

Series of five spray-painted track-bike frames, 2009.
Client: MWM Graphics
Photographer: Matt W. Moore
Page 206

Mural, 2009.
Client: MWM Graphics
Photographer: Justin Keena
Page 206

Series of three posters, 2009.
Client: MWM Graphics
Page 207
—

MEREDITH LEWIS + ALEX NEUMAN
www.nowheresoon.com

Nowhere Soon, 200.9
Photographer: Meredith Lewis
Pages 44 – 45
—

MICHAEL DELUCIA

Of Primitive Means, 2009.
Photographer: Bertrand Huet / Tutti Image
Pages 132 – 133
—

MICHAEL EIDE
www.yakkay.com

Designers: Claus Jensen, Henrik Holbaek (Tools Design),
Morten Langebaek (I•U•V•O), Marianne Tuxen (Mari-
anne Tuxen Industriel Design), Maria Berntsen
Manufacturer: YAKKAY
Page 110
—

MICHAEL UBBESEN JAKOBSEN
www.baubike.dk

BauBike, 2009.
Page 53
—

MIGUEL LUCIANO
www.miguelluciano.com

Pimp my Piragua, 2009.
Photographer: Jehangir Irani
Page 174
—

MONKEYLECTRIC
www.monkeylectric.com

Page 86
—

MONOVELO
www.monovelo.com

Monovelo, 2009.
Page 84
—

N

NIHOLA BIKES
www.nihola.de

Family, 2001.
Designer: Nihola Bikes
Client: nihola germany GmbH
Photographer: Barbi Mlczoch, www.barbimlczoch.de
Carlos Labraña A.
Page 175
—

**NORMAN HAYES (WASTE) WITH
DANIEL LOWE (DLOWE)**
www.wasteyourself.com
www.dlowe.co.uk

Fixie Death Trap, 2009.
Page 130
—

O

**O2 SPORTS MARKETING / NORTH
AMERICAN HANDMADE BICYCLE SHOW**
www.handmadebicycleshow.com

Various, 2009.

[1]
Designer: Richard Sachs
Manufacturer: Richard Sachs
Photographer: Brad Quartuccio, www.urbanvelo.com

[2]
Designer: Jason Montano
Manufacturer: Broakland
Photographer: Brad Quartuccio, www.urbanvelo.com

[3]
Designer: Jordan Hufnagel
Manufacturer: Hufnagel Bicycles
Photographer: Brad Quartuccio, www.urbanvelo.com
Pages 182 – 183
—

OGYAN
www.rintendo.com

[1]
Robin, 2000.
Manufacturer: Tsunoda

[2]
Jokee, 1996.
Manufacturer: SHUKUNO-RINTENDO
Pages 54 – 55

[1]
Firetrick Bob, 1997.
Manufacturer: SHUKUNO-RINTENDO

[2]
Aquatrick Bob, 1997.
Manufacturer: SHUKUNO-RINTENDO

[3]
Gaap Street, 2003.
Manufacturer: KUWAHARA

[4]
Gaap Tour, 2004.
Manufacturer: KUWAHARA
Pages 56 – 57
—

OLIVIER PASQUAL
www.olivierpasqual.ch

Bike, 2009.
Client: The *Club Voice* magazine n°35 / Swatch AG
Photographer: Olivier Pasqual 2009
Magazine layout : Superposition (Geneva, Switzerland)
Pages 170 – 171
—

OVERTREDERS W
www.overtreders-w.nl

Pixelpoort, 2009.
Designers: Overtreders W (Reinder Bakker and Hester
van Dijk), Maartje Dros, Eric Klarenbeek
Client: Zaanstad City Council
Photographer: Jorn van Eck
The project was commissioned by Zaanstad City Council.
Pages 142 – 143
—

P

PAPER BICYCLE
www.paper-bicycle.com

Paper Bicycle on Jetty, 2009.
Paper Bicycle in Glasgow, 2009.
Paper Bicycle in Glasgow, 2010.
Photographer: Nick Lobnitz
Page 145

Bicycle trailer.
Page 159
—

P – S

PARLEE CYCLES
www.parleecycles.com

Parlee Z1, 2009.
Designer: Bob Parlee
Manufacturer: Parlee Cycles, Inc.
Page 195
—

PASCULLI
www.pasculli.de

PASCULLI, hand-made frames.
Photographer: Timm Kölln
Pages 101 – 103
—

PAUL ELKINS
http://highmileagetrikes.blogspot.com

Various, 2006, 2009.
Photographer: Paul Elkins and others
Pages 50 – 51
—

PAUL SMITH
www.paulsmith.co.uk

Paul Smith & Rapha, 2007.
Page 14

Paul Smith Kashimax saddle.
Page 112

Paul Smith and Mercian Cyles, 2006.
Manufacturer: Mercian
Page 209
—

PEDRO REYES
www.pedroreyes.net

Ciclomóvil, 2008.
Photographer: Mark Powell
Client: Museo de la Ciudad de México
Page 52
—

PROJECT LE TOUR
www.projectletour.com

Bike on Lawn, 2005.
Photographer: Brent Humphreys for "Project Le Tour",
www.brenthumphreys.com
Page 16

Bike Pyramid, 2005.
Photographer: Brent Humphreys for "Project Le Tour"
Page 17

Project Le Tour, 2007.
Photographer: Brent Humphreys for "Project Le Tour"
Page 100
—

R

RADIATOR ARTS
www.radiatorarts.co.uk

Radiator Arts at Skyride, 2009.
Designer: Adam Thompson
Photographer: Adam Thompson
Page 76
—

RANDALL STEVENS
www.madeinqueensfilm.com
www.randallstevenscreative.com

Made In Queens, 2008.
Designer: Future Shock
Photographer: Randall Stevens
Pages 29 – 31
—

RAPHA
www.rapha.cc

Paul Smith & Rapha, 2007.
Page 14

Pages 105 – 107
—

RECOAT GALLERY GLASGOW
www.recoatdesign.com

"Spin on This" exhibition, 2009.
Page 34
—

REW10
www.rew10.com

REW10 tall bike Yokohama Special, 2009.
Designer: Yanaken & Ryuji Ikeda

REW10 Daruma, 2009.
Designer: Ryuji Ikeda
Page 67
—

RICHARD MITCHELSON
www.richmitch.co.uk

Rouleur T-shirt designs, 2009.
Client: *Rouleur* magazine
Manufacturer: Rapha
Page 98
—

RICHARD SACHS
www.richardsachs.com

AtmoSawa, 2007.
Photographer: Jeffrey Weir
Page 195
—

ROBB MEERTENS
www.robbmeertens.net
http://www.flickr.com/photos/beatznbobbz

Bike Polo.
Pages 36 – 37
—

ROBIN LEY
flickr.com/raytracing

Various, 2009.
Photographer: Robin Ley
Pages 74 – 75
—

ROXY ERICKSON
www.roxyerickson.com

Tweed Run, 2009.
Photographer: www.roxyerickson.com
for Brooks England
Pages 18 – 21
—

S

SARAH ILLENBERGER
www.sarahillenberger.com

Super Bicycle Highways, 2009.
Photographer: Reinhard Hunger,
Picture Editor: David Carthas
Client: The *New York Times Magazine*
Page 15
—

SCHINDELHAUER BIKES
www.schindelhauerbikes.de

2009.
Manufacturer: Schindelhauer Bikes
Photographer: Florian Grill
Page 144
—

SEVEN CYCLES
www.sevencycles.com

Bike Book, 2009.
Photographer: Anvil Tegelaar
Page 194
—

SIMON PEPLOW
www.simonpeplow.com

[1, 3, 4]
Exhibition pieces for Sprocket Rockets, 2009.
Client: Superb Bicycle Boutique

[2]
Coca-Cola / 2012 London Olympics skateboard presentation, 2009.
Client: 2012 London Olympics – Coca Cola
Page 24

S – Y

5
Fausto Coppi, 2009.
Client: *Anorak* magazine

6
Jaques Anquetil, 2009.
Client: *Anorak* magazine

7
Eddy Merckx, 2009.
Client: *Anorak* magazine

8
Braveheart, 2009.
Client: *The Ride Journal*, UK
Pages 24 – 25
—

STEVIE GEE
www.stemagency.com
www.dustywolf.blogspot.com

Vengeance is Coming!, 2009.

1,4,5
Photographer: Stevie Gee, dustywolf.co.uk
Built by tourdevillelondon.blogspot.com
Painted by deathspraycustom.com

2
Photographer: Stevie Gee, dustywolf.blogspot.com

3
Photographer: Stevie Gee, dustywolf.blogspot.com
Sewed by Sarah Parker,hereiamtheresheis.blogspot.com
Screen-printing Stu:lovenskate.com
Pages 210 – 211

6
Photographer: Anthony Dickenson, Stem agency
Built by tourdevillelondon.blogspot.com
Painted by deathspraycustom.com
Plinth and frames by shapeconstruction.co.uk
—

STUDIO TRACTOR
www.studiotractor.com

Cotter Pin bicycle rack, 2009.
Designer: Peter Kirkiles, Mark Kolodziejczak,
Michael Tower (Studio Tractor with PKDF)
Photographer: Studio Tractor
Architecture PLLC
Page 155
—

SWOON
www.wearechangeagent.com

boy-on-a-bike.
Page 77
—

T

TEUN VOETEN
www.teunvoeten.com

Chukudu, Goma, 2009.
Photographer: Teun Voeten
Page 159
—

THE BUNGALOO
www.thebungaloo.com

Stork Legs on a Penny Farthing, 2009.
Client: Screens 'N Spokes
Page 136

The Last of the GhettoBlasters, 2009.
Client: "ARTCRANK"
Page 137

THE K.I.D.S. AND SECRET SCHOOL
www.kidsociety.wordpress.com
www.secretschool.wordpress.com

2
Growing a Network of Secret Gardens, 2009 – 2010.
Designer: The K.I.D.S. and Secret School
Photographer: Huong Ngo
Page 118

The Portable Pantry, 2007.
Page 119
—

U

UNCOMMON PROJECTS
uncommonprojects.com

ybike, 2008.
Client: Yahoo!
Manufacturer: Uncommon Projects
Electronics and software: Uncommon Projects
Case design: Hyde Power
Bicycle: Electra
Concept: Yahoo! Buzz
Photographer: Kevin Meredith
Page 151
—

V

VANMOOF
www.vanmoof.com

2009.
Page 147
—

W

WIL FREEBORN
www.wilfreeborn.co.uk

Bicycles = Good, 2009.
Page 43
—

WILL MANVILLE
www.willmanville.com

Photographer: Patrick Kim
Page 42
—

WORKCYCLES
www.workcycles.com
www.bakfiets-en-meer.nl

1
Trash-collection bakfiets, 2004 – 2010.
Designer: WorkCycles
Photographer: Henry Cutler, WorkCycles
Page 176

2
WorkCycles Fr8 Family, 2008.
Designer: Henry Cutler
Photographer: Nijland
Page 176

3
Classic Dutch bakfiets, 2005 – 2010.
Photographer: Henry Cutler, WorkCycles
Page 176

4
Family tandem, 2002 – 2010.
Designer: Ronald Onderwater
Photographer: Martin van Welzen
Page 177

5
WorkCycles cargobike long, 2001 – 2010.
Designer: Maarten van Andel
Photographer: Martin van Welzen
Page 177
—

WOUTER MIJLAND
wouter-mijland.com

Bakfiets and *Limousine*, 2008.
Photographer: Wouter Mijland
Page 62
—

Y

YIKEBIKE
www.yikebike.com

YikeBike, 2009.
Designer: Grant Ryan
Photographer: YikeBike
Page 148
—

BICYCLE CULTURE
AND DESIGN

EDITED BY ROBERT KLANTEN AND SVEN EHMANN
TEXT BY SHONQUIS MORENO AND OLE WAGNER

COVER BY FLOYD SCHULZE FOR GESTALTEN
FRONT COVER PHOTOGRAPHY BY J. ADELAIDE MÉTIVIER, DAVID GWYTHER, ANTHONY DICKENSON, ALEX LEE
LAYOUT BY FLOYD SCHULZE FOR GESTALTEN
TYPEFACES: FRANK PRO BY ANTON STUDER. FOUNDRY: WWW.GESTALTEN.COM/FONTS
NOBEL BY TOBIAS FRERE-JONES, SJOERD HENDRIK DE ROOS. FOUNDRY: WWW. MYFONTS.COM

PROJECT MANAGEMENT BY ELISABETH HONERLA FOR GESTALTEN
PRODUCTION MANAGEMENT BY MARTIN BRETSCHNEIDER FOR GESTALTEN
PROOFREADING BY ENGLISH EXPRESS
PRINTED BY GRAPHICOM SRL., VICENZA
MADE IN EUROPE

PUBLISHED BY GESTALTEN, BERLIN 2010
ISBN 978-3-89955-284-3
2ND PRINTING, 2010

It also has been printed according to the internationally accepted ISO 14001:2004 standards for environmental
protection, which specify requirements for an environmental management system.

Gestalten is a climate-neutral company and so are our products. We collaborate with the non-profit carbon offset
provider myclimate (www.myclimate.org) to neutralize the company's carbon footprint produced through our world-
wide business activities by investing in projects that reduce CO_2 emissions (www.gestalten.com/myclimate).

DZINE   Custom lowrider bicycle, 2009, Detail.
24 ct gold plating, chrome, enamel, Swarovski crystals, rubber,
and mirror. Courtesy of the Leeahn Gallery, South Korea.